Why Teach History?

Pamela Mays

University of London Press Ltd

ISBN 0 340 05362 3 Boards
ISBN 0 340 05361 5 Unibook

University of London Press Ltd
St Paul's House, Warwick Lane, London EC4P 4AH

Printed in Great Britain by
Hazell Watson & Viney Ltd
Aylesbury, Bucks

Contents

Acknowledgments

The author and the publishers would like to thank the following for permission to reproduce illustrative material in this book: The Trustees of the British Museum for the four German wood-cuts which are reproduced on page 60; Macmillan Education Ltd for the picture of crowded houses of the industrial age, from *History Picture Book 5 A, Victorian Times to World War I*, page 2; Mr David Pepin for a page from his booklet *Let's Explore St Alban's Abbey*; Pictorial Charts Educational Trust for the wall-chart 'The Tudors' reproduced on pages 92–3; Thomas Nelson and Sons Ltd for the page from *Citizenship for School Leavers, Book 1—The Family*, by M. W. Thomas, reproduced on page 143; and ESL Bristol for a part of the wall newspaper *Focus 39*, issued 2 April 1973, reproduced on page 145. The photograph on page 97 is reproduced by courtesy of the B.B.C.

The photographs of models and of children's drawings were taken by Mr Brian Long from models prepared by the author and her pupils and students, and from drawings by Robin Mays. The book on dinosaurs was made by children of St Stephen's Primary School, Richmond, Surrey.

I
Why Teach History?

Today, history as a subject in schools is under attack, and for several reasons. To many people, and to young people in particular, it seems out of key with the age in which we live. For one thing, ours is not a society which apparently reveres the past, for in such a quickly-changing technological age any lessons of the past possess little relevance. The whole atmosphere of our times is impatient, seemingly wholly loving the present, too absorbed in its own problems to be bothered with what has gone before. Then, too, in a technological society, relying on technical skills to produce the standard of living with which it is so intensely preoccupied, a philosophical, meditative study like history appears to have little to offer. Many are the times when a child will say to a teacher, as I have had said to me, something like, 'Have I *got* to do history? It won't get me a better job, will it?' This little girl was putting into words the common feeling that, as history teaches you no particular skill, it is of very little use.

Other, more subtle forces are at work, and these reflect both a change in our values and a change in our ways of communication. The value of history has always lain in the old liberal values, in the respect it teaches for balanced judgement, fairness, caution in reaching conclusions. The thinking of historians has always been expressed in words, indeed one might say that it can be expressed in nothing else. Yet one sometimes feels that these ancient values now have little meaning. This can be sensed in the class-room, seen in the faces of the sixth-formers patiently taking notes on great historical issues that one suspects mean nothing to them. History seems to be asking the wrong questions, and receiving irrelevant answers. Further, the medium in which history must be expressed, words, seems sometimes almost in disgrace. People are used now to other easier and superficially more attractive modes of communication. Often they distrust words. How then can one teach a subject whose ideas must be expressed in verbal concepts? Many a teacher finds him- or herself faced with a class to whom words like 'parliament', 'liberal', 'the manor' mean nothing, and who find great difficulty in thinking about them.

To many people, indeed to many teachers, it seems more sensible to replace history in the schools with a course of social studies, or civics. These courses, it can be argued, are far more relevant to the needs of today's children than a study of the past. This argument carries considerable weight, particularly as our society is now so complex that many of its citizens feel lost in it. Sadly, large sections of the community, as social workers will tell, are completely ignorant of their rights and of the help they can get when in need, and many more have little sense of responsibility towards their fellows. Surely it is more important for the schools to prepare children for their future responsibilities than to worry about the past? Many schools are in fact doing this. Civics and social studies are becoming more and more popular and history correspondingly less so.

The teaching of history in the schools is under attack from yet another quarter. There are those, historians and teachers among them, who believe that it is too difficult a subject to teach young children. It requires mature judgement, careful balancing of fact, meticulous attention to detail, abilities which children do not generally acquire until approaching adolescence. It should not be taught, it is argued, because it is impossible to teach it properly.

Then there are intellectual trends, excellent in themselves, which seem to detract from the value of history as a subject in its own right. One of these trends is the increasing popularity of integrated studies. Knowledge is indivisible, it is stated; there should be no hard and fast lines between the subjects, they should be taught as one. This is absolutely true, but such an approach can, in practice, mean that no subject is taught particularly well, or for itself.

In the face of all this opposition, it seems to me vitally important that history should continue to be taught in the schools, and taught as itself, not watered down or made 'attractive' by teaching it as part of civics, or by teaching it backwards, or indeed in any other way. I hope to discuss one aspect of history which has been little explored, and that is its relationship to the mental and emotional development of children. It seems to me that the teaching of history can actually encourage the development of a child's mind in very important ways. I hope also to show that history can teach children a great deal about their society which cannot be learnt in any other way.

One must begin, however, by a discussion of what history as a subject is, otherwise its nature as a teaching subject cannot be seen.

Like all the mental disciplines that form part of our intellectual heritage, history has a very long history itself. The word 'history' literally means a story, or a record, and taken in this simple, narrow sense, the earliest peoples in the world can be said to have written history. The Ancient Egyptians who, thousands of years ago, carefully recorded the height of the Nile each year were writing it; the Red Indian notching up his number of scalps on his tomahawk was writing it; each one of us writes it when we keep a diary, or, in our own heads, reflect and meditate on the events of each day. One might say that the historical process comes naturally to the human mind.

While societies remained simple, history too remained a simple matter, but at a certain point in the evolution of civilisation it becomes infinitely more complex. This point seems to be when the people in a society became aware of themselves as having a separate identity from other groups, a degree, if you like, of national selfconsciousness. It also comes when a society reaches a certain stage of economic development, partly in specialisation and partly in wealth, so that it is able to free some of its people from physical drudgery and can afford to support a class of artists and intellectuals. People then begin to think about the origin of their society, its important events, and the values which make them different from others. The historian then becomes a kind of interpreter and spokesman for his people. He has a social function. This is the kind of history that is written in western society today.

There is obviously much room for disagreement as to exactly when this type of history came to be written. The Ancient Greeks may, perhaps, claim to have been the first in western civilisation to express a national identity. Certainly the Romans followed. In Britain, rather a late developer in some respects, this kind of history may perhaps be said to emerge with Francis Bacon's *Henry VII* in the sixteenth century, though, of course, chronicles had been written before that.

At this point, we ought to consider what the historian's task is, and how he works, for this shows us what kind of subject history is. Suppose our historian is interested in a particular subject, say the plague in England in the sixteenth century. He will probably have read everything that has been written about his subject by other people; in fact he may have been led into a desire to do his own research by something said by one of them, or by some aspect of the subject that he feels needs further investigation. Books written about a subject in this way are called secondary sources.

Having formed a shrewd idea as to the line of research he wishes to pursue, our historian will then track down all the primary material he can find. There will be records and descriptions written by people who actually lived in the sixteenth century, perhaps portraits painted of those who are to figure in the study, even objects such as furniture or such medical equipment as existed in those days. All these are called primary sources. Possibly our historian is in possession of some new primary material, documents or letters which he thinks will throw a new light on his subject.

People often assume that such sources are easy to come by. This, however, is often not the case. Evidence there may once have been, but it may have been destroyed. Again, it may be that the people of a given time were so hard-pressed and illiterate that all their time was taken up in the sheer struggle for survival so that they left few records. This is often said of the 'Dark Ages', the period following the fall of the Roman Empire, and a period notoriously difficult for historians. Sometimes a historian knows that sources exist, but he is not allowed to have them. An individual's family may not be at all anxious to hand over his private letters, or to have painful facts about him revealed. Sometimes a government is tempted to destroy, forge, or falsify

3

records for political motives. If a historian finds that there is insufficient primary material, for any of these reasons, he may have to abandon his research. Alternatively, he may find there is too much material to be dealt with, and have to modify his work for this reason also. This particuarly applies to twentieth century history.

However, if our historian is lucky, and meets with none of these difficulties, he can then begin his work. It is important to realise what goes on in his mind when he begins, for on this rest several weighty questions as to the nature of history as a subject. One of these questions is: how far can the historian be truly objective and what is the nature of historical truth? In some ways the historian works as a detective and a scientist, tracking down evidence and assembling facts. But a moment's reflection shows that wherever he makes a judgement, however trifling, he ceases to be objective. These judgements have to be made all the time. We are all accustomed to think of facts as hard and immutable, but even the decision as to what is a fact is subjective. Still more so is the decision as to what facts to present. Take my day today, for example. I got up at 7 a.m. and cooked bacon and egg for breakfast. But why have I chosen to tell you this? Many other things were happening. The day was windy; I had three letters and the post-man walked across the front lawn to deliver them, trapping his fingers in our new letter-box. I could go on for ever. What governed my decision to tell you about the bacon and egg—a decision taken quickly and without deep thought? Now I come to think about it, I told you this because it seemed important to me; it must have done, as it was the first thing to come to my mind. Also, I knew that these kinds of facts are understood by everybody. I was taking into consideration your response, and I had at the back of my mind, not only my own interests, but a sort of instinctive knowledge of the kind of information that is considered relevant in our social context. To select, then, is to be subjective, and the historian selects all the time.

When the historian comes actually to assess people and events, he is being more consciously subjective. He must, of course bring into play his own experience of life, what appeals to him, what he thinks important, every time he makes a judgement. A history book can therefore never be a list of 'facts'. It would be meaningless, and quite valueless, if it were.

One must remember one other thing. The historian is a man of his time. The values of any society are continually changing, and its mental disciplines, and what is considered important within these disciplines, change with them. Economics are considered very important nowadays, for instance, and political and constitutional history can even be presented in terms of economics, but this has not always been the case. A history book written in Victorian times might well be found to consist of political events only.

Amusingly enough, some of the great figures of history suffer a variety of fates according to the views and prejudices of the age in which their histories are written. Oliver Cromwell is a good example of this process. Directly

4

after his death, when the Stuarts returned to the throne amidst great rejoicing, Cromwell was described by contemporary writers as a kind of anti-Christ. Later, he faded into insignificance and was considered scarcely worth a mention in English history—the Protectorate was just an unfortunate interlude. In the nineteenth century, with the increasing popularity of Republican ideals in certain quarters, Cromwell became a hero once more, an early upholder of democracy. In our own day he has become, not exactly a hero, because heroes can hardly be said to exist any more, but certainly an exceptional figure and an interesting psychological study.

And so Cromwell has passed through many vicissitudes at the hands of historians. He has been written about by men and women who were creatures of their own age, and who were influenced by ideas and mental climates of which they themselves were scarcely aware.

A history book, then, whether it is written for a child of six or a man of sixty, can be described as an interpretation of the events of the past. Historical truth is never to be found in any one of these interpretations, but rather in a grasp of all the interpretations available at one particular time. Historical truth is always changing.

For some reason, many people find this very disturbing. So do children. 'This book doesn't agree with what you said!' they will cry accusingly to their teacher. Even older students can be cast into despair at the discovery of two interpretations of the same events. The human mind seems to hanker after an infallible, certain, easily obtainable truth. Such a thing does not exist in real life and it does not exist in history either. One can sometimes get this across to a group of children by the following game. Ask everyone to write a short account of some experience they have had in common. It may be the morning school assembly, or you might like to devise some amusing little occurrence for them as you enter the room. Then get everybody to read out what they have written. Each account will be different. In the same way, and for much the same reasons, historians differ when they write history books. This is what makes history such a fascinating and rewarding subject.

However, although most people would agree that this is so, there are many teachers among them who believe that history is too difficult a subject to teach to young children. There is a strong school of thought that believes that history should not be taught before adolescence, because it requires a maturity of thought and judgement that a young child cannot possibly possess. While no one would expect a young child to make the kind of historical judgement that must be supported by mature intellect and an adult experience of the world, nevertheless I believe that this is to take too narrow a view of history. I believe that history teaching, like the teaching of other subjects, should be closely related to the development of the child's mind. There is, as yet, no broad philosophy relating the teaching of history to child psychology, but I believe that, when this is done, it can be seen that history has a vital part to play in the intellectual and emotional development of the child.

I would like to make a beginning in the second half of this chapter on 'Why teach history?'

First, though, one must make the general observation that it is possible to teach all subjects at different levels. One level is no more valid than another; it is just different. One cannot, for example, teach higher mathematics as it is taught at university to a seven year old, but it has been clearly shown in recent years that children of this age can grasp, and enjoy, fundamental mathematical concepts. It has been shown that they can learn a second language at this age, without detriment to the still incomplete knowledge of their own. It all depends on how they are taught. The teaching of any subject must go hand-in-hand with the particular stage the development of the child has reached, otherwise, the brutal truth is that it is better left untaught.

What, then, has history to offer the young child in his struggle towards maturity? The first thing it has to offer him is people.

It is true to say that one of the most important aspects of a child's development in its first few years is his increasing awareness of people, and of the importance of human relationships. When a baby is born, he is, at first, only aware of himself. In his first two years of life the young child learns to identify, first, his mother, then his father, then brothers and sisters. By about two he is aware that there are people outside his own family—those all-important figures of childhood like the milkman, the dustman and the coalman. One might almost say that at this stage he has one of the prerequisites of an understanding of history, for he is aware, in an unspoken way, that society exists. Slowly he becomes aware that people exist even outside his familiar, everyday figures, and by about six or seven he knows that there are lots of people in the world. Television, with the fascination it holds for children, helps to bring about this awareness earlier than ever before.

Everybody knows that the world of a little child of two is people with characters. Some are real, some are not. There are real people, imaginary people, animals, trees, natural forces like the wind and the moon—everything is seen in terms of personality. This is partly because the young child does not yet know that there are different kinds and degrees of life and therefore assumes that everything lives and feels in the same way as himself—it is also the child's way of teaching himself about life. By animising the wind, the thunder, and so on, he can come to terms with them, for he makes them like himself. The point for us here is that young children under five can learn about life through people. Now when one presents people to children, even at this tender age, one is teaching them much that is very valuable, much more than the simple fact of their existence. One is teaching them about human nature, its reactions to certain predicaments, its wickedness, its goodness, and also tacitly imparting the values of our own time. Take two hoary old stories of early childhood: King Alfred, who burnt the cakes, and King Canute, who tried to drive back the sea. These are both favourites with little children, and one suspects that much of their popularity is due to the fact that both are telling, fascinating comments on human nature.

This curiosity about human nature persists. Anyone who has taught children of seven onwards will be aware that they often know far more about the personal lives and habits of famous people than one does oneself. They know about all the wives of Henry VIII and especially how they were executed, all about the symptoms of the plague, all the details of the toilette of a fine lady of the eighteenth century. And if they do not know already, to offer such scintillating information is a sure way of ensuring their rapt attention.

One hardly needs to labour the point that this interest persists throughout adult life. The popularity of the gossipy family serials on radio and television are ample testimony to that. People and their doings, and everything about them, are of vital interest to us from cradle to grave.

It is important to realise that children learn far more than idle gossip when they learn about people in history. They are learning about past society, and also about their own. When they hear about King John of Magna Carta, they are learning about the nature of political power in the Middle Ages, how it could be used by one individual, and the sanctions mediaeval society imposed in order to control him. When they hear, at the other end of the scale, about Lord Shaftesbury in the nineteenth century, they learn from his life the problems of a different society, of the response made by one man, and the impact he made.

Children learn to make judgements when they learn about people, because people always invite judgements to be held about them. In this way they learn something yet more subtle, and that is the moral valuation of their own time. When a group of children discuss, say, Oliver Cromwell, they are hammering out what they mean (and what their own society decrees they shall mean) by words and phrases like 'ruthless', 'a family man', 'dictated to by circumstances', 'religious', and so on. The meaning of all these words and phrases has changed over the years. Think about them, and you will see that their meaning has changed radically even in the last ten years. Constant reassessment is necessary, and when we, or the children we teach, make these reassessments in discussion, we are adjusting to the social values of our own time.

Through learning about other people, children also learn about themselves. That is, in fact, how all of us learn a great deal about ourselves. It is only when John notices that Mary dislikes games that he becomes consciously aware of the fact that he himself does like them. In learning about the people of the Middle Ages, he can say to himself, 'My life is not like that; I have different things to eat; I can read and write. I am different.' If he reads about a great man in history, say Napoleon, he can, perhaps, tell himself, 'I admire that man. He was brave and clever. That is what I would wish to be myself.' History can make a child more keenly aware of his own identity.

As a child becomes more strongly aware of his own identity, so he finds it easier to draw the line between fact and fantasy. This problem of the fantasy element in a little child's thinking has an important bearing on the teaching of history. At what age can a child distinguish between what actually happens in the world and what happens inside its own mind, between fact and fiction? Is there any point in teaching history before it can make this distinction? History, after all, is about real events, and real people.

I would like to take the first question first. In my opinion, to ask at what age children can distinguish between fact and fiction is to put the matter too crudely. It is much more subtle than that. Even very small children can distinguish between what is happening in their own minds and what is going on in the real world. Young babies are well aware that the source of food and comfort lies outside themselves, and their crying is a way of making contact with this source. Those of us who are acquainted with two-year-olds know that some time during its second year a child starts to enjoy make-believe games. It pretends to go shopping, to go to work, to be the butcher or the milkman. It picks up objects and makes them do as other things—a stone for a milk bottle, a book for a joint of meat, so that it can carry on the game. Its behaviour, its obvious enjoyment of the game, show clearly that it has grasped the distinction between fact and fantasy. It does not think for one moment that it is really engaged in these pursuits, or that its book is really a piece of meat.

On the other side of the picture, even adults retain a strong fantasy element in their thinking. We all have our day-dreams. Any police officer will tell you how the witnesses of an accident invariably differ widely in the accounts they offer. This is not because they are dishonest, it is because their inner minds intrude upon the outward event.

Because young children show that they perceive the outside world, and because mature people are still very much involved with the inner one, it seems to me that we are not really discussing the ability to distinguish between fact and fantasy at all, but something else. This is the ability to apply appropriate modes of thinking to certain groups of facts. Let me explain further. It seems to me that human beings are capable of various modes of thinking throughout their lives, almost from birth, but that what they learn from experience is the ability to apply these kinds of thinking appropriately. For example, if one heats a metal ball it will expand. It is no good pretending it will not. Here a scientific mode of thinking must be employed, for one's end will be defeated otherwise. But if one were creating a visual fantasy for, say, a film, one could have objects defying all the laws that apply to scientific thinking—floating about, shrinking, changing colour, because here one's aim would be different and one is thinking differently. One is trying to reach a different kind of truth.

Children learn to think appropriately as a gradual process, over the years. This is a long and complex development, involving many factors. At some point during early childhood a child's physical senses become developed enough to provide a point of reference between it and the outside world. A moment's thought will show that this must indeed be true, for if we had no senses of sight, hearing and touch we could not possibly distinguish between ourselves and the world around us. At the same time, as the child grows more fully aware of itself as a person, it can draw the line more confidently between fact (the outside world) and fantasy (the inner one).

What bearing does all this have on the teaching of history to children? To my mind, it means, not that young children should not be taught history, but that they can gain a great deal from it, at a much earlier age than is often assumed. Just because history is about the real people and the real events of the past, it can help children to reach mental maturity. By the time they are about eight, most children are mature enough to avoid confusion on this score, but if they are not, one can rest assured. It will come in time.

Teachers of children between the ages of five and eleven, and even beyond, find one other great difficulty in the teaching of history. It is that children of this age-group often seem to have no idea of historical time. It is difficult to get them to realise how long ago, say, 350 years is, so that, to the bemused teacher, it seems that the eleventh, seventeenth and nineteenth centuries are all the same to them. They often think that their teacher was an intimate friend of Queen Victoria, or (a very interesting error in thinking), because no people were alive at the time of the dinosaurs, that dinosaurs could not really have existed. Or, when told a story about the past, they reproduce the events all out of order. An interesting example of this, reproduced overleaf, are the drawings with captions that a seven-year-old boy made of the Battle of Bunker Hill.

It is important to realise that this apparent confusion is but the normal process in the very orderly development of the child's mind. In any case, what do we mean by the phrase 'historical time'? Upon examination, this apparently simple term turns out to be highly complex.

Let us consider first how the young child's sense of time develops. A baby lives entirely in the present. When it is hungry, its hunger is all there is in the world, and so its grief is all-consuming. However, as its brain develops, it can form a pattern of memory. It can then remember that, in the past, its need for food has been met. A mother of a baby of six months can often calm it by telling it that she is getting its food ready and it must wait a little. The baby may then wait patiently (but not for long!), secure in the memory that in the past she has kept her promise. It has developed a sense of time.

The toddler comes to grips with somewhat wider problems; those like 'yesterday', 'tomorrow', 'this afternoon' and 'this morning'. Many is the time when the three-, four- or five-year-old, and sometimes even a nine-year-old, will be uncertain as to whether an event took place in the morning of a particular day, or the day before. 'Did that happen only this morning?' they will cry. 'I thought it was yesterday!' It is significant that, in this context, children invariably think that something happened longer ago than it actually did. This is because they are so sensitive and aware that each impression makes a great

The Battle of Bunker Hill, drawn by a seven-year-old boy

impact. No sooner is one impression received than it is superseded by the next, the former being cast into oblivion—the far-distant past. Children of this age have not yet developed the capacity to set these impressions into an abstract pattern, as adults do, which automatically lessens the impact, and their minds can only retain a certain amount at the same time. Even adults are familiar with the same experience, for we all know how, after a day of earth-shaking events, we feel that we have lived through an age.

Some time between the ages of five and eight, a child jumps the next great hurdle. He comes to realise that other people have been in existence before he was born. It is a long time before this is accepted completely. How many times does one hear a child of this age say cheerfully about an event of the past, 'Oh, that couldn't have happened! I wasn't born then.' Until a child reaches a certain stage in his mental development, he sees all life as existing in time simultaneously. However, he does eventually grasp that time is not synonymous with consciousness, and that lives have been lived before his own. It seems to me that a child first comes to realise this through observing his own family. It dawns on him that his parents are older than he is; he hears them talking about events that happened before he was born; perhaps there are grand-parents who can tell of an even more distant past; there may be younger brothers and sisters who can't remember things the child in question can. Above all, the child comes to realise that he is changing all the time himself—he is surprised to find that he has grown out of last year's clothes, that he can climb the tree that he could not before. He learns that, with the passage of time, things change.

An interesting point arises here. Many a child has difficulty in synthesising all these existences into one abstract, all-embracing pattern of time. I knew a little boy of four who, though unable as yet to tell the time, took to wearing as many toy wrist-watches as he could find, all the way up one arm. I asked him what they were all for.'This,' he said, pointing to one watch, 'is for meal-times, and this,' pointing to another, 'is for going home, and this,' pointing to yet another, 'is when the dustman comes.' 'They are all different times,' he explained. He kept each watch for a different person or event, for he had not yet come to realise that all events and all people exist in the same concept of time, and that one watch would have done.

Having accepted, reluctantly, that there exists a past in which he cannot share, the child enters upon the next stage, usually between the ages of six and ten. This can be hilarious, for he assumes that anyone older than himself can remember everything. He has not yet grasped the complexity of existences in time, he simply sees his own existence and the past stretching beyond it. Children of this age often assume their teacher actually knew Sir Walter Raleigh or Queen Elizabeth in person. It causes considerable amusement.

However, by the time they are about eleven years old most children have quite a good idea of historical time. They fully accept that there is a past, that people lived and events took place before they were born, and during different periods.

This realisation is vital to the teaching of history, and the teacher can help the development of children's time-sense greatly by the right approach. The first essential is to accept children's apparent difficulties in this respect for what they are—as the normal stages in a child's mental development. They are not a reason why history should not be taught to young children, rather are they a very good reason why history should be taught, and taught well. Then the teacher of young children can present the past to them in such a way as to develop their time-sense. For example, if you are talking about the eighteenth century, you can help them to envisage how long ago this was by putting it in terms of their own families. Most children in the class will have a grandfather. He will probably be somewhere in his fifties, so the eighteenth century is roughly four or five grandfathers back. You can draw the grandfathers on the board, or get the children to. Talk slowly, for this takes time to sink in.

Another attractive idea is to paint a road all the way round the walls of the class-room. Divide it up into centuries, or periods of time, then the children can paint or stick people, houses, animals, villages and so on in the appropriate spaces. This gives them a very good picture of how things have changed, and this sense of change is, after all, at the very heart of historical thinking. It is just as important as grasping the mere fact of time.

Another way of helping to develop children's time-sense is to have a Time-Clock. There are various ways of adapting this idea, but basically you cut a large circular piece of cardboard and fix a hand at the centre. Round the

The clock tells the time: 1650

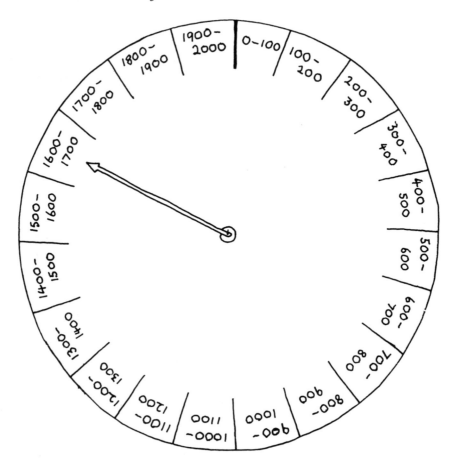

circumference you mark the centuries, or, if you are talking about one century, the single years. You move the hand of the clock to point to the year or the century you are talking about. Each child can make his own clock, and use it by himself. This idea can be further refined by making a clock with two hands. If you are dealing with, say, the fifteenth to the twentieth centuries, you can have the hour hand pointing to the centuries and the minute hand pointing to the single years.

We are probably all familiar with the most commonly used kind of time-chart, which is made simply by allotting so much space on a piece of paper to each century, and filling in the great events and people appropriate to each space, as shown in the illustration on page 14.

These ideas lend themselves to almost infinite adaptation, but the object behind them is the same. It is to enable the child to grasp the concept of something abstract, such as time, by reducing it to what can be seen and easily grasped, like a space on paper.

Two things always need to be simply explained to children: the way in which we divide up the past into centuries, and the way in which we use the terms A.D. and B.C. They often find, for example, it very hard to accept that, say, 1909 is in the twentieth century, and not in the nineteenth. It is also puzzling for them to find that 125 B.C. is further back in time than A.D. 30. With young children it would not, of course, be necessary to bother about using these terms ('so many years ago' would be enough), but when you feel they are ready to understand these conventions, explain them clearly and repeat your explanation at intervals. They will know that, if they are eight years old, they are actually in their ninth year, and they can apply the same reasoning to centuries.

I would like now to return to a point I mentioned at the beginning of this discussion on children's time-sense. It is the way in which children often seem to get historical events completely out of order. The best examples I have come across of this apparent lack of historical thinking are the drawings of a seven-year-old boy of the Battle of Bunker Hill. These drawings have been reproduced on page 10. He was told the story of the Battle, and then he decided to reproduce it in drawings with captions underneath. His first picture is called 'Awarding the Medals'. Then comes 'Getting Ready for the Battle', after that 'The End'. Then, unexpectedly, comes 'During the Battle', followed by 'The Beginning', and finally 'Hot in the Battle'. What sense does all this make?

I think the answer is that this little boy was being completely logical in his own mind, for he was simply putting the most important things first. To a boy of seven, awarding the medals was by far the most important thing about the Battle of Bunker Hill, so that came first. Then, having dealt with the end, his mind swung logically back to the beginning of the fight, then back yet again to the more formal ending, with all the soldiers lying dead. Having reached this point, I suspect that this little boy must have paused. Having

A TIME-CHART COMPARING THE CIVILISATIONS OF ANCIENT EGYPT, GREECE AND ROME

Dates	Egypt	Ancient Greece	Ancient Rome
5000–4000 B.C.	4241 The Egyptians learn how to make a calendar.		
4000–3000 B.C.	3300 They develop hieroglyphic writing.		
3000–2000 B.C.	2500 The Great Pyramid is built at Giza.		
2000–1000 B.C.	1887–1849 Sesostris III makes Egypt a great military power. 1955–1912 lived Hammurabi, the great law-giver.	1500 The Mycenaeans establish the first civilisation in Greece. 1000 onwards, the rise of the City States, Athens and Sparta.	2000 A farming people settle on the Latin plain near the River Tiber.
1000 B.C.–A.D. 1	The Egyptian Empire begins to decline. 670 Egypt is invaded by the Assyrians. 525 Egypt is invaded by the Persians.	500–400 was the golden age of Greek culture, of science, drama and the famous philosophers, Socrates and Plato, 431 but war breaks out between Athens and Sparta. 146 Greece becomes a Roman province.	753 Rome is founded. 509 Rome becomes a Republic 60–44 Julius Caesar, the famous general, rules. 58–49 Caesar sends expeditions to Britain.
A.D. 1–1000	A.D. 30 Egypt becomes a province of the Roman Empire.		27 B.C.–A.D. 14 The Emperor Augustus reigns. The Roman Empire is established and lasts until A.D. 476. Jesus Christ is born at Bethlehem. A.D. 43–83 The Romans conquer Britain. A.D. 180 Roman power begins to decline. A.D. 455 Rome is destroyed by the barbarians.

The Battle of Hastings, drawn by a seven-and-a-half-year old boy

dealt with the really dramatic episodes, he was then free to think about the rest. The last three pictures are really careful studies of the actual fighting—you can see that they are depicted in much greater detail than the first three. The more one looks at them, the more dramatic and packed with action they are seen to be. His pictures are really a very good account of the Battle of Bunker Hill, even though he was thinking in episodes, rather than in strict historical time.

Children often think in this manner. One would not wish to alter this way of thinking; indeed one cannot, for it is natural to children. They come, in time, to have the mental discipline, and the desire, to record events as they actually happened in time—less intelligent children take longer to achieve this than others, and one can find backward adolescents still producing work like this young boy.

One should remember a related point here. It is that often what is to an adult a sequence of events based on logic is in fact what has been learnt by experience. After all, we expect the sun to rise in the sky each day, yet few of us could prove by logic that it is bound to do so. We have learnt this sequence of events by experience. Similarly, the way in which events seem to follow upon one another in history is something we come to learn, and we may well find ourselves attributing strange quirks of thinking to a child when, in fact, all he lacks is experience.

Teachers of history are often troubled by yet another kind of inaccuracy on the part of the children they teach. Take a look at the picture of the Battle of Hastings reproduced above. This is by the same boy who drew the Battle of Bunker Hill. He is now seven and a half. Again there are the same quickly drawn but vivid fighting-men; one can sense the despair of the losers and the aggression of the little group of Normans in the bottom left-hand corner.

A battle between Saxons and Vikings, and one between Romans and Britons, drawn by a seven-year-old boy

However, pride of place in this picture of an event in 1066 is taken by what appears to be a fighter-plane of World War II and a twentieth-century anti-aircraft gun. If you had asked this little boy whether such things really existed in 1066 he would have replied 'No'—he knew they did not. To him it would be a silly question. But he put these things into his picture because, to him, this aeroplane and this great gun epitomise war and all that goes with it. He was simply borrowing the externalia of one age to express what he felt about another. There is no real inaccuracy here.

Actually, this boy of seven shows a very sound grasp of historical detail, as children of this age often do. Take the picture above, also drawn when he was seven. He knows that the Saxons and Vikings had sailing ships with square sails, that they fought with bows and arrows and spears, that they carried oars on their ships and fought at sea by boarding the enemy vessel. In the lower part of the picture, he shows that the shields of the Romans were quite different from the round, smaller shields of the Britons; he draws the crested Roman helmet accurately, and, from the expressions on their faces, he shows that he knows the Romans won! He really knows a lot of history.

This discussion of a young boy's drawings perhaps enables us to define further what we mean by historical time-sense. It involves not just a sense of time passing, but something much more subtle. To begin with, it quite clearly involves the association of certain facts with the appropriate period in history. What jars in the little boy's picture of the Battle of Hastings is the presence of the fighter plane and the anti-aircraft gun. We know they do not belong to that period in history. On the other hand, we automatically note with satisfaction the accurate way in which he has drawn the Saxon ships and the Roman soldiers. We know that these details belong. This relevance is carried far beyond mere physical detail in the study of history. We would expect a mature student to place modes of expression and ideas in their correct historical setting. We would not, for example, expect him to place the Darwinian theory of evolution in the sixteenth century.

This ability to place facts in their correct historical setting is a complex matter. It is partly a matter of sheer experience, but behind it lies the development of a whole mental complex about a particular age, the association of its events with its ideas, ways of expression and philosophy.

At what age can children form such a complex? There is no short answer, for they begin when they hear their first story and continue throughout life. I think it is true to say that children begin by forming a complex involving concrete, physical detail, such as the clothes people wore and the houses they lived in, and proceed, as they develop, to include the more abstract, ending with the really abstract, such as philosophy. I think it is also true to say that those of greater aptitude form richer and more subtle complexes than the less able, and go on enriching these for much longer. Many an adult finds it quite within his grasp to remember the clothes people wore in seventeenth century England, but quite beyond it to understand the doctrinal disputes of the same period.

We can then further define what we mean by historical time-sense. It involves a sense of the appropriate.

Yet another concept forms part of the sense of time in history, and this is an awareness of cause and effect, a sense of development. We see an 'event', the Industrial Revolution, say, as having had 'causes', such as improvements in transport, expansion of trade, a supply of labour and so on. Equally, we think of it as having had 'effects', such as the replacement of the domestic by the factory system, the suffering of certain classes of people and increased production of goods. An awareness of the relevance of these factors is part of one's grasp of history.

Although this is a useful way of thinking because it helps us reduce facts to order, and therefore to draw conclusions about them, it should be used with care. This approach tends to assume an inevitability about historical events which many historians would claim did not exist. The conditions to which we fondly attribute the coming of the Industrial Revolution might have suffered a change at any moment in time, brought it about differently, or not at all.

However, in spite of its pitfalls, the concept of cause and effect is part of the historical thinking of our age, and we expect children eventually to grasp it. It is part of thinking in time. In my experience, this kind of thinking only comes with maturity. Young children think in episodes; like the little boy who drew the pictures, they make rich associations, but they do not think in terms of cause and effect until approaching adolescence. This, of course, affects our approach to the teaching of history, but once again it is no argument for not teaching it.

Perhaps we are now in a position to draw some conclusions as to how we can define children's sense of historical time. It implies, firstly, a sense of the passage of time in the physical sense, a realisation that there is a past and that people lived in the past. This children gain by about eight. Then it implies an acceptance of the way in which historical events take place chronologically, and a willingness to give this type of thinking precedence over other types. This the little boy who drew the pictures was as yet unable to do, but one would expect him to do so by about ten. While a child is developing these abilities he is also developing his sense of time by a process of association. He is learning to associate facts with their appropriate period in history, starting with the concrete and proceeding to the abstract. This process goes on throughout life. Finally, the adolescent, approaching mental maturity, learns to think in terms of cause and effect. He can then be said to have achieved a sense of historical time in the fullest sense.

This brings us to the conclusion of our chapter. Why teach history at all? The first reason is that we can never really escape history. It is part of our lives, part even of every individual's way of thought. History has a lot to give us all, though this may be different in the case of each person. It cannot give us an infallible yard-stick by which to rule our lives, hanker though we might after such an easy way out, but it can give us many things even more valuable —an idea of the many-sided nature of the truth, perhaps a sense of what is transitory in life and what remains unchanging. It helps us to understand human nature. To the child, history and its discipline is of great value. It is a natural help to him in his normal intellectual and emotional development. It teaches him about himself, and about the society in which he lives. It can help him over some of the hurdles he must clear in order to reach mental maturity.

2
The Approach, the Story and the Book

Fifty years ago everyone knew what to expect of a history lesson. The teacher stood in front of the class by the black-board, chalk in hand, while the children sat before her in straight rows. The teacher talked, while the class listened. As an alternative to this oral teaching, which would consist entirely of the doings of kings and queens or of notable men and women, the children might read from their text-book, taking it in turns to read round the class. Learning by heart was the inevitable piece of work set from both these exercises.

Nowadays the picture is quite different. There has been a flood of ideas concerning the teaching of history and there are many ways of teaching it attractively. There is, for example, model-making, and the introduction of original sources to children, until a few years ago considered too difficult for them. Pictures, films and broadcasts, which fifty years ago would have been considered undesirable distractions, are now not only freely used, but considered essential to good teaching. Local history has become increasingly popular, and so has the integration of history with other subjects. The 'text-book' is somewhat in disgrace, implying as it does some infallible source of history; the teacher, surveying the hive of industry in the class-room and work proceeding happily without her, must often feel likewise, or at least uneasily uncertain as to what her role should be.

A great change has taken place in educational thinking and this has inevitably affected the teaching of history. All the recent approaches have one thing in common. They are child-centred, aiming at enabling the child to learn through its own activity. This being the case, one ought to consider what activities come naturally to the children of any particular age-group. Can one, for example, say that at a certain age a child is likely to enjoy group-work? When is he likely to be able to write an essay? I think it possible to make some generalisations, albeit with very great care. I had, for example, always been taught, and always believed, that it was typical of the very young child that he could not think abstractly. Then one day a six-year-old came up with a group of interested friends and asked, 'Which is the greater, infinity or numberless ?' They had been arguing about it. You could hardly have a more perfect grasp of the abstract than that implied in the question, and these were not particularly 'clever' children.

However, having recounted this incident, I must say that I think it was unusual, and that children of this age usually are more interested in the concrete than in the abstract. Suffice it to say that no one knows all there is to know about human nature, or about children, and that when one chooses one approach rather than another, one must do so in true humility and with an open mind.

The very young child, say the one found in an infant class, has certain characteristics. He is first and foremost a very busy little person, immature and physically vulnerable in many ways, yet possessed of tremendous energy and never really still. His hands, particularly, are always busy. He asks continual questions, even though he is not, as yet, in complete mastery of his native tongue; his questions are penetrating although his world is a small one and his horizon narrow. He cannot yet concentrate for long, and certainly he will not sit still and listen to anyone for more than about ten minutes. If he is very young he may often live in a world of fantasy, believing, for example, that if he wants something to happen, it will happen. He lives very much in the present, the past and the future being too far away to matter, but he does know there *is* a past.

Certain ways of teaching history to a small child like this suggest themselves. He will love all kinds of stories, for these will appeal to his imagination. They will also help to develop his sense of time and sequence. He will love making things—big dramatic models that are not too complex for his still imperfectly co-ordinated hands. He will not be able to read and write much by himself, but hearing about what has happened in the real world will help him to distinguish between fact and fantasy and will satisfy his intense interest in the little things of life.

Between eight and twelve, children are physically at their most energetic. I state this first deliberately, because so often this essential fact is ignored in the class-room. Much so-called 'naughtiness' is because these children simply have not enough outlet for their physical energy. Neither is sitting at a desk the most comfortable position for them. Left to themselves with a book in their own homes they invariably stand or lie down to read it. It almost seems, sometimes, that many class-rooms could not have been better designed to make these children uncomfortable had they been deliberately thought out for this purpose. The teacher of history should remember these things. Any approach that gives the child freedom to move, or indeed to go for a good long walk, as in local history or an environmental study, is a welcome one.

As well as being physically very active, these children have a great sense of adventure. They, too, love stories, but only where things 'happen'. I once listened to what I thought was a charming story with some children of this age-group. It was all about a kettle coming slowly to the boil, and while it did so the room gradually darkened, the cat stretched and woke up, until in the end it was tea-time. That was the end. I listened entranced, but the children felt cheated. 'Is that all?', they cried. 'Nothing happened!' Had the house caught fire, the cat been rescued by the fire-brigade in the nick of time, and hidden treasure discovered behind the curtains, they would have been satisfied. The point is that these children see things in an extrovert way, events mean external events only, and physical events at that.

Children of this age are intensely interested in everything around them. They like to know how things work, all about the details of other people's lives, and their curiosity seems endless. They also love to work with their hands. Watching these children, unable as yet to think abstractly, it is almost as if they actually think with their hands and bodies. Asked a question, their faces change, they wriggle, they move their hands and feet—they react with the whole of their bodies. Their senses are also acute, so that pictures, colours and sounds make a great impact on them. They love to paint and model.

At this period of their lives children like to work with each other. Much of their spare time is spent in each other's company; school over, they rush out to play games, walk round the shops, visit each other's homes, but nearly always in a gang. Group work, therefore, comes naturally to them.

So far, the eight to twelve-year-old has seemed from this description an extrovert, outward-looking creature. It is important to realise that behind all this outward activity he is also inward-looking. Children of this age are at their most imaginative, and, what is more, have embarked on that long process of finding themselves which ends only with full maturity. Any way of working that stimulates their imagination is valuable. History can also help the child to realise his own identity by presenting him with some of the people of the past and letting him dramatise some of their great moments.

The eight to twelve-year-old has a great advantage over his younger brother. He can read and write. The handling of words is a vital part of mental development, and this not only enables his teacher to offer him a wider range of work, but, because history is largely itself a literary subject, work done in this field will help him in all others.

The child of this age has also a much better historical time-sense than the younger one. His sense of the past is richer and more subtle, and he accepts the fact and complexity of existences in time before his own. However, he has still not reached mental maturity. He has difficulties in thinking of the kind described in the previous chapter and he can be greatly helped by teaching along the lines suggested.

This age of childhood, when a child has stepped beyond babyhood and yet has not reached the perplexities of adolescence, is a delightful one. He responds equally well to all approaches in teaching and is usually a joy to teach.

The adolescent presents rather a different picture. Our society depicts the time of adolescence as a period of emotional and behavioural crisis, and it is true that these children often present a great problem to their schools.

So far as history goes, a boy or girl from thirteen onwards usually has to cope with examinations, and these dictate the whole approach to teaching, usually for the worse. Apart from this, the adolescent has special needs of his own. He reads very much to find himself, to associate himself with an adult role and to think about his future in society. History can help him here, and so can courses in civics and social studies. Above all, the adolescent needs time, time to think and reflect, and this he is rarely given. He likes discussion, for having by now a good mastery of language and being able to think logically he enters on what seems to the adult an age of incessant talk. Adolescence is the time when the world is put to rights and earth-shaking questions asked in endless, earnest talk with friends or a kindly adult. It is as the latter that a teacher comes in.

The adolescent can also write well and he likes to work by himself, or with a friend; more rarely now will he choose to work in a group. His historical sense is nearing maturity, for he can think logically and abstractly and he will have amassed a fair historical knowledge. He is less interested in modelling, unless it is as a strictly intellectual exercise with everything to scale, and he does not need the constant stimulus of visual aids because he can carry ideas in his head. Discussion, writing and reading seem to be the natural ways of working for the adolescent boy or girl.

One must remember, however, that adolescents vary very greatly from one another in ability; there is a greater range among them than in any other group. If one is teaching children who at fourteen can hardly read and write, other methods must be used. Children who are below average in ability can usually be taught in the ways used with younger children, though one must be careful, in this case, to see that the subject matter interests them. It is no good teaching a backward fourteen-year-old boy about King Alfred and the cakes, merely because the story happens to be written in simple language.

I think, then, that it is true to say that some approaches to the teaching of history are more appropriate to the children of particular age-groups than others. I think that this will emerge even more clearly as we proceed with a more detailed discussion of these approaches, and what they have to offer.

The story is perhaps the most popular way of teaching history. It has a great and universal appeal for children of all ages. Often such teaching begins long before the child goes to school, from the very first moment his mother or father begins 'Once upon a time . . .'. This popularity continues right through childhood, and, indeed, right through life. Reading remains a source of enjoyment and information, of a richer level of existence, for the vast majority of the population. What, then, is the appeal of the story?

Firstly, I think its appeal lies in this very richer level of existence that we cannot find in our everyday lives. Many things can be expressed in the written word that cannot be expressed otherwise. There are nuances of emotion, patterns of life, sadnesses and strange joys of personality that pass unnoticed in our day-to-day existences. The written word can convey them all, not just for the people of the present, but for the people of the past too.

For children, the story has a special significance because it is written in time. It always has a beginning, a middle and an end. This applies to all stories, whether fact or fiction, and whether they are about history or any other subject. In this sense, any story told to a child is the beginning of history teaching, for the one essential about history as a subject is that it concerns human experience in time. Then, too, the story helps children to distinguish between the world outside themselves, and the world within, the distinction that is often crudely described as between fact and fiction. The constant telling of stories to children, of whatever kind, helps them draw this line more clearly.

Apart from these vital considerations, the story is the vehicle of much that is rich and important. It introduces the child to a variety of characters and a wealth of experience that may fall right outside his own life. Mentally, he is drawn to thinking about all this, to drawing conclusions about people of the past and their lives, and about his own life, which in turn enable him to hammer out standards of behaviour and to make judgements. Often the story is a subtle way of transmitting the values of other civilisations. Take, for example, the myths the Greeks wrote. The stories of Echo and Narcissus, of the wanderings of Ulysses, are a far more senstivie way of transmitting the values of that ancient civilisation than any abstract talk by a teacher. The beauty of stories of this kind is that they can simply be read or told to children and need no further comment. Indeed, to comment often spoils them. This means that even little children can imbibe history, though lacking, as yet, the capacity to verbalise.

Little children cannot concentrate for long though, and they usually cannot listen for more than about fifteen minutes. Their stories should not be confined to English history, or even to Western civilisation, for by telling them stories of other civilisations, they can be led into an intuitive appreciation of peoples whose lives and achievements have been different from our own. They come, early in their lives, to accept other cultures, and this is very important in the world today. As they grow older and reach the middle years of childhood, from about seven to thirteen, children turn more and more to adventure stories. The ten-year-old wants to hear about all that is exciting in history, and particularly about the exploits of great men and women. There is a reason for this, for this is the age when he is seeking his own identity, and he can measure himself against the people of the past. The young adult, or adolescent, has an enormous range of reading. He still likes adventure stories, but he is also more introspective and can think abstractly. Most kinds of story appeal to him.

Often, one has to decide how to present a story to a class. Shall one tell it, or read it, for example? Small children usually prefer to be told a story rather than be read to, and there is a very good reason for this. To be told a story is part of their relationship with their teacher. The story is a gift, and is taken as an expression of her love and concern for them. Even much older children like to be told a story, and anyone who has told a story to a class knows what a warm, happy occasion it usually is. Nevertheless, sometimes children should be read to, or read by themselves. The reason for this is that every individual has a characteristic way of speaking, with typical idiosyncrasies. If you find this difficult to believe, try analysing the speech of yourself and your friends, not only the number of nouns, verbs and adjectives you use per sentence, but also the rhythm of your sentences, and the rise and fall of your voice. It follows that if you only ever tell a story to your children, you are confining them to one style of language—yours. Ideally, they should have the opportunity of listening to many styles of speaking, many ways of constructing a sentence, and this you can give them if you read from a selection of authors. It should also be remembered that the spoken word is quite different from the written one, and that children need to hear both.

Publishers have long recognised the appeal of the story as a way of teaching history and there are many chronological history books, textbooks, if you like, written in story form. Incidentally, the Historical Association (for address, see page 154) publish an excellent pamphlet, 'Story-telling—Notes for teachers of history in the Junior School', from which a teacher can work up his or her own stories, re-telling them in simple language.

History books in story form often centre on the lives of notable people. I can only mention a few. A. and C. Black, Harrap, Chatto and Windus, and Oxford University Press all produce series of this kind. Each series consists of three or four little books, telling about the lives of the famous people in a particular period. They range from ancient to modern times, and they can be enjoyed by children of from five to thirteen, the younger ones having the books read to them.

Pergamon Press in 1964 embarked on a new venture, the *Awake to History* series. This is a complete history course over four years for slow children in primary schools, but it could equally well be used in secondary schools. The course consists of chronologically arranged series of stories from world history, the books progressing in difficulty of language. In Book 2, for instance, no sentence is longer than eighteen words. Accompanying each volume are supplementary readers for children to read by themselves, a book of playlets for them to act and a teacher's book so that she can answer all the questions!

It seems to me that a series of this kind takes full account of the classroom conditions and the educational theory which influence the teaching of history today. It recognises that less able children must be taught differently from the quicker workers, that there should be a variety of activity in any one lesson, ranging from the children reading and acting for themselves to the oral lesson given by the teacher. It makes possible a variety of ways of organising the class.

Another very popular series is the Ladybird books. These are brightly illustrated, inexpensive books, ranging from simple stories for the very young to exciting adventure stories for older children. Many of these, too, centre on the exploits of one great man or woman.

Several publishers produce biographies specially written for children. Harrap have produced a whole series, ranging from *Great Discoverers in Modern Science** to a series on the saints. Macmillan and Oxford University Press produce similar books.

Although stories about the great men and women of English history are by far the easiest to obtain, it is very important that every teacher should find time to hunt down books about civilisations other than our own. They are many and vivid, and are being increasingly published. One can always start by looking at the shelves of the public library.

Perhaps the richest source of all of the history of other cultures is to be found in the myths these people have created about themselves. Myths are imaginary stories, half-based on truth, written by people for their own amusement. They cannot possess the factual accuracy of other kinds of story, but they reflect the values of their civilisation in a way that no straightforward factual account ever can. They should be simply to read to children for themselves. Any comment, unless asked for, turns appreciation into an impossibly difficult intellectual exercise, whereas most of this appreciation takes place on a non-verbal level. I would like to mention some of the more unusual myths of other lands that can be used in history lessons. There is *Myths of the Norsemen*, edited by Roger Lancelyn Green, published by Penguin, and Ginn produce the *Myths of the Red Children*, consisting of eighteen tales of the American Indians. One should also look to the literature of the Far East. W. H. Allen publish a lovely book, *Tales from Japan*, which has vivid pictures, while Bodley Head produce volumes of fairy tales from fifteen countries, including England, Germany, Japan and Sweden, in a series called *Favourite Fairy Tales*. The stories told by the Chinese and Russian peoples are comparatively easy to come by.

One would not wish to omit the myths of Britain—the stories of King Arthur and his knights, of Robin Hood, and of Dick Whittington. We also have our nursery rhymes. All these transmit in a magical way the atmosphere of the times in which they were written.

We have discussed the factual story in the history lesson, and also the myth. Another kind of story is being written today, and this is the imaginary reconstruction of the past. C. M. Rutley has written a number of books of this kind. Eileen and Rhoda Power's *Boys and Girls of History* (Dobson) and *More Boys and Girls of History* (Cambridge University Press) are well-known examples of this kind of book. The advantage of reconstruction is that it enables the author to incorporate a great deal of accurate historical detail

*Not all the titles listed in this chapter and elsewhere in this book are still in print, but most can be found in school or public libraries.

without being bound by what actually occurred in a given period. The characters are often children. These books are ideal for children to read by themselves as background.

The story, then, the oldest approach to the teaching of history in the class-room, remains a widely accepted and imaginative way of bringing the subject to life.

Just as widely used as the story-book in the history lesson is what is known as the textbook. I refer to it in this somewhat tentative fashion because when I was at the beginning of my own teaching career, one of Her Majesty's Inspectors remarked to me, 'There are no such things as textbooks, only books.' I have pondered over this ever since. Is there such a thing as a textbook? Can it exist in its own right, or is it just an inferior kind of book? I have come to the conclusion that there is such a thing as a textbook, and that it has its place in the history lesson.

One thing I am sure will be accepted, and that is that the history textbook has greatly changed its character in the last ten years. Once upon a time, the textbook used to be a matter of cramming as many unappetising facts as possible into small, unattractive print. Illuminated by a few spidery drawings —not too many in case the reader's attention should wander from the text —it was wedged firmly between hard grey or dark brown covers. The book of today is a very different affair. It is likely to be gaily produced with vivid pictures and pleasing print, and written in a style that invites one to read it. This revolution reflects the change that has taken place in education, namely its child-centredness. We no longer expect the child to adapt himself to history, we expect history to adapt itself to the child. However, in spite of these striking changes, I think it is true to say that the textbook retains its essential characteristic; that is, it aims at presenting an objective body of fact. It is this impartiality that makes it a valuable teaching aid. Rightly used, it should act as a jumping-off ground for all sorts of interesting, stimulating work.

Unfortunately, the textbook is probably the most abused of all the teaching aids. In my own school-days our history lessons consisted of reading round the class, a paragraph each, a chapter per lesson. To be caught reading on ahead on the sly was to merit being kept in. The same state of affairs exists in many schools today.

It is therefore worth while considering why we use a book at all in the history lesson. What actually *is* a book? The answer must be that it is in the nature of a book to be a transmitter of ideas, and in transmitting these ideas it makes the reader reach out to form his own. A book should never be used as an end in itself, for this kind of procedure closes up the mind. It should never be used as a vessel of the absolute truth, the sole source of information, for this makes a travesty of a critical subject like history, in which the truth is many-sided. Neither should any book (or anything else) be used as a substitute for the teacher, who must always accept the responsibility for teaching. It should be used actively, as a stimulus to thought and imagination, and it should be used critically, together with other varied sources of knowledge.

To enable children to use a textbook actively, one should always set them an objective. It may be that they have in their minds questions they are going to answer. If they are reading about William the Conquerer, they may be asking themselves, who was William the Conquerer? Why did he come to England? How did he prepare for his journey? Perhaps some of the questions can't be answered from the book. In that case, all the better, the answers will have to be searched for somewhere else. Or perhaps the objective will be of a different kind. Perhaps pupils are going to prepare short talks on some aspect of the subject, or perhaps a group of them may dramatise it. Or it may be that they are going to produce a piece of written work.

Many teachers feel uneasy when it comes to setting written work from a textbook, and often the work set is dull. The most common problem is of children who are too young to write much, or who may be illiterate. Learning to read and write fluently is a vital part of learning history, a subject whose ideas are conveyed in words, and for the young or backward there are various ways of encouraging this.

Perhaps we can take our cue from the way in which a child learns to write, and the stages he goes through. He learns to draw long before he can write, so it is a good idea to encourage him to write through his drawings. Even a young child can draw William the Conqueror landing in England; a slightly older child will be able to add to it a picture of the Battle of Hastings, then William being crowned. He will then have the essence of the story in three pictures. If these pictures are produced in comic strip form, he can, helped by the teacher if necessary, write a sentence or two beneath each picture— 'William lands in England', 'William fights Harold', 'William is crowned'. He has then written a little history of his own. Children like working in this way; it is the way chosen by the little boy whose work is reproduced on page 15.

There comes a time when a child can dispense with pictures, but he still needs help with writing. He will still be incapable of writing sentences, or of writing at any length by himself. At this stage it is helpful to him if his teacher writes the story on the board, or on the work-card, leaving gaps for him to fill in, first single words, then a phrase or two, and finally his own sentence. Thus:

———— the Conqueror came to England in ————.

The ———— gave him his blessing.

William came to England because ————.

He fought King ————.

This is how ———— was killed in the Battle of Hastings.

Children take to this with great glee. Sometimes one can write the appropriate words in a column beside the paragraph. If they are all jumbled out of order the children enjoy it even more. There are many amusing variations of this kind of written work.

Children from about the age of eleven onwards will be ready to begin writing simple historical essays. It is worth while discussing with them what an essay is meant to be, for it is quite a different kind of writing from the narratives they will have been used to until now. An essay is an exercise in thinking, it involves forming an opinion, weighing evidence and making judgements. The hallmark of the story, that it concerns a sequence of events in time, is missing from the essay, and this children frequently find hard to accept. Even with students it is often a herculean task to convince them that what they have written is not an essay, but a story. The transition from narrative writing to the essay form should, then, be a gradual process, leading from one to the other. This transition can be made orally at first, by, for instance, picking out a point of interest in a story and discussing it with the children. Is there only one point of view about the invasion of Anglo-Saxon England by the Normans in 1066 ? What did the Anglo-Saxons feel about it ? Discussion of this sort will lead children into balancing view against view, towards thinking in essay form even if they cannot write in it. When, later, they come to writing an essay, planning it with them and writing interesting points on the board will greatly help them.

However, it is not the essay that is most frequently set as a piece of written work from the textbook, but the taking of notes. At first sight, setting the class to make notes of the textbook has attractive advantages for the teacher. It needs little effort on his part; each child has to work by itself, so that it is a peaceful exercise for which silence can be imposed; there is always something to show at the end of it (or usually anyway) and the work can be easily assessed. Furthermore, with the increasing pressures of examinations, which now dog the lives of all children not only the more intelligent ones, note-making seems to be the only possible way of covering the syllabus. Against these apparent advantages must be set the overwhelming truth that taking notes is usually a dreary, inactive way of working, leading, at best, to a lot of meaningless information learnt off by heart. It can effectively prevent a child from thinking at all, let alone developing his own historical judgement.

Yet there is still a place, an important place, for the making of notes as an historical exercise for children, provided that it is seen for what it really is. Making notes from a textbook should be seen as an intellectual exercise, a matter of analysis. It is an indispensable tool for anyone who progresses beyond an elementary level in any subject. For this reason children should learn the technique. It is really the art of selecting the important. Further, the mental effort involved in making this selection greatly aids the memory. Where it goes wrong in the class-room is that it is imposed too suddenly, and without explanation. Note-making should be introduced gradually, with a great deal of discussion, so that it comes as a natural development of a child's thinking. It should be used in combination with a variety of other approaches in the teaching of history.

The making of notes and the writing of essays are usually exercises given to older children. I should like at this point, therefore, having discussed in the first chapter and in the beginning of this one the problems of the young child in learning history, together with the approaches that may prove useful, to consider some particular difficulties experienced by teachers of older children.

In the first place, as has been said, boys and girls in their teens differ much more widely from each other than younger children appear to do. If the class is unstreamed, the teacher may face boys and girls of high intelligence, together with those who are far below average. Some of the difficulties in teaching such children in one group may be overcome by the use of work-cards and study-kits. These are described in chapter 6 on the organisation of the class. There remains, however, one particular problem, and that is the question of books for the backward older boy or girl. As has already been pointed out, the adolescent with breaking voice or sudden surging interest in make-up and boy-friends does not take kindly to childish stories written for the eight-year-old. There is a great dearth of the kind of history book that can be used by the backward teenager, that is, the book that contains adult subject matter but which is written in simple style.

Two suggestions may prove useful here. The first is that it is possible for the teacher to make up his or her own history readers for the less-able children, using pictures cut out from newspapers and magazines (the Sunday colour supplements are a good source), and writing a simple text underneath. Even better is to encourage these children to learn history by making their own books. I have found that they respond to this eagerly if they now that their work is going to be used in some way. I once asked a backward group of older boys and girls if they would help the younger ones in the school by making them some simple books on 'difficult' subjects like the Agricultural and Industrial Revolutions. These were actually subjects that I thought the older children should know something about. They responded to this joyfully, learnt a great deal in doing so, and their work found a respected place in the class libraries of the younger children.

Apart from differences in intellectual ability, adolescent children differ from each other in their interests, attitudes and individual style of doing things. Their great need is therefore for variety, particularly in books but also in ways of working.

So far we have discussed the story-book and the textbook and their uses in the history lesson. The 'patch' and 'line of development' approaches are two other popular ways of teaching history, and for both these publishers are producing a wealth of material. 'Patch' history is the study of one period intensively, to give a many-sided portrait of an age. One often sees 'patch' studies being carried out in schools on subjects like Prehistory, Elizabethan England, and the World Wars. Suppose one were intending to work in this way on Elizabethan England. One would perhaps spend a whole term on it and cover all aspects of life during this time: economic problems, how people lived, the religious settlement, Queen and Parliament, the great explorers, art and drama, and so on. There are obvious advantages to this kind of work. Firstly, it is, in fact, how life must have been lived in the past. The Elizabethan would have been the living embodiment of these things, they were part of his daily life, affecting the food he ate, the work he did, his family and his worship. As this, then, is how life was lived, surely it is how history should be studied.

Further, as every teacher is faced with the problem of selection anyway, what better way of solving it than by embarking on a series of well-thought-out 'patch' studies, so that the children can imbibe the very atmosphere of those times? Even if it means that other periods of history must be left out, the children will at least gain some idea of what real historical study means. 'Patch' history also inspires children to a variety of individual and group-work. Following such a study in depth, some will want to model, others to act out their own drama, some to carry out a further investigation of a particular point. All this arises quite naturally.

In spite of its vivid appeal, 'patch' history in the classroom has its drawbacks. For one thing, it worries teachers that, taken to its logical conclusion, 'patch' history would mean a series of intensive studies with nothing in between. This would surely mean that the children would lack a sense of historical development, apart from knowing nothing at all about various vital periods in our history. 'Patch' history, then, should not be used to the exclusion of other approaches. I personally am in favour of using it within the framework of chronological history, as a means of encouraging children to work in depth. It needs, too, to be introduced in conjunction with a time-chart, or at least care should be taken that the particular period is set in historical perspective.

'Patch' history also calls for a wealth of appropriate reference books and materials that children are able to use by themselves. It also needs a properly planned room. This is where so many 'patch' studies fall down. It is quite impossible to expect children to carry out an intensive study of a period when there is a scarcity of materials to work with. Not only is it important to provide the appropriate books, but the classroom should be planned in such a way that these are easily accessible so that children who want a particular source of reference can fetch it without disturbing everyone else.

Provided these conditions are met, the 'patch' approach to history is a very rewarding one. Contrary to what many people believe, quite small children can benefit by it. Children who cannot read can work from pictures. For many years, Macmillan produced excellent sets of *History Class Pictures* in colour. These pictures were of a size to be pinned on the wall, or studied by a group, and to accompany them the publisher issued individual booklets which contained smaller copies of the large illustrations, with a simple text underneath each picture. By studying the pictures, or grouping them together in subjects, the young child or the one who cannot read can make an interesting many-sided study of a particular period.

At the time of writing (April 1973) the large-scale pictures are going out of print, but most of the smaller *History Picture Books* are still available, and *Book 5A, Victorian Times to World War I*, will be referred to again later.

Other picture series that can be used for class teaching in much the same way are put out by various publishers. There is a lively series of ten profusely illustrated books in the *Wayland Pictorial Sources Series* (Wayland Publishers); the books cover great events in world history, from *The Dawn of Man*, through *The Voyages of Discovery*, to *The Russian Revolution* and *Twentieth Century China*. The same publisher issues the *Eyewitness History Books*, for nine to thirteen-years-olds, covering Tudor to Victorian times, and *Wayland Picture Histories* for older children, illustrating topics such as the trades union movement, Parliament, and industrial trades and crafts up to the dawn of industrial times.

Brockhampton Press has produced a series of *Picture Reference Books*, specially useful for children who cannot cope easily with the written word. Each contains many captioned drawings and photographs, on some subjects as many as three hundred. There are over twenty titles available, on subjects such as the Saxons, the Middle Ages, Costume, and Aircraft, and they are very reasonably priced.

Then there are the *Picture Source Books for Social History*, published by Allen and Unwin. As an example of what is offered, the *Picture Source Book* for the twentieth century contains ninety-six pages and eighty-two photos. So one need not despair if the children with whom one wants to carry out a 'patch' study are unable to read, whether because they are too young, are backward, or are perhaps immigrants. They can use other kinds of material, mainly illustrative. They may not be able to write much about what they have learnt, but they can act out a little play, produce a scrap-book, or simply arrange the pictures and talk about them. Who knows, they may be inspired to burst into writing, as I have seen happen many a time.

Some very good books are produced for children who can read. I cannot mention them all, but I would like to mention some suitable for younger children, as these are often difficult to find. Macdonalds publish a *Junior Reference* Library, aimed at children between the ages of six and twelve. These books range across all the subjects, including history. Then there is Blackwell's *Learning Library*. This consists of simple books about interesting topics of the present day, with a great deal of historical background. There are, for example, books on *Policemen and the Police Force, Fires and Firemen*, and *Postmen and the Post Office*. The *History Bookshelves*, published by Ginn, are little reference books specially for children. They are simply written, yet contain such useful information that they can be used by children of all ages. As the *Bookshelves* cover definite historical periods, they are particularly suitable for patch sutdies. They come in various colours according to the period they cover, and each set has a teacher's booklet. Somewhat similar little 'patch' books are produced by Longman in the *As We Were* series, booklets on such subjects as *A Norman Castle 800 years ago*, and *A Seaside Town 130 years ago*. Children love these books.

For children between the ages of eight and thirteen there are the *Then and There* books, also published by Longman. These are excellent; there is a wide range of titles, many on 'patch' studies, and the same firm is now producing film-strips to accompany the books, thus adding a new dimension to the written word.

If one likes the 'patch' way of working, one can find history textbooks which are arranged as a series of 'patch' studies. R. J. Unstead's books in the *Looking at History* series (Black) are examples of this kind of approach. There are volumes on *The Middle Ages* and *Tudors and Stuarts*, and each book is set out in the form of 'patch' studies of the clothes, the modes of travel and the food of the time.

A valuable source of reference books for studies in depth of a particular subject, often overlooked, is Her Majesty's Stationery Office. The Stationery Office regularly publishes excellent pamphlets on specialised subjects. There is one on *Arms and Armour*, for instance, which is a mine of information.

The 'patch' study can provide children with an opportunity to use books and pictures in conjunction with a wealth of other material. There are the B.B.C. and I.T.V. broadcasts, both on sound and television, many of which aim to throw an intensive light on one problem or theme. There are also study-kits and collections of original material, specially prepared for children, which are ideal for use in a 'patch' study. Children find these other sources of material very illuminating when used in conjunction with a book.

There is, then, a wealth of books and material available for children to use in the 'patch' study in history. It remains for the teacher to ferret them out and make them easily accessible.

Another interesting way of studying history is to examine, not one particular period in depth, but the evolution of a single trend throughout a length of historical time. One might, for instance, take clothes or transport, from the beginning of history to the present day. This is called 'line of development' history, and in many ways it is directly contrasting to the 'patch' method. Whereas the 'patch' study gives an intensive knowledge of a particular period, the 'line of development' way of working should impart a sense of long-term evolution in time. It is, in fact, a widely used way of working in the schools, among children of all ages.

It is widely used because, firstly, it is a simple way of teaching history. It is particularly useful with young or backward children, for the obvious reason that this kind of study does not require masses of historical detail, as the subject matter is automatically limited to whatever one is studying, be it ships, or houses, or clothes. 'Line of development' history also lends itself to the use of a variety of visual aids, in themselves a great help to the slow learner. For these reasons, the 'line of development' study is much more widely used in the schools than 'patch' history.

In spite of its obvious advantages, this way of working has its drawbacks, and these should always be carefully considered. Behind 'line of development' history there lies a particular historical philosophy with which one may not agree if one thinks at all deeply about it. It implies, for one thing, the inevitability of progress. If one is working on the evolution of the ship, one sees how the ship progressed from strength to strength through the ages, increasing steadily in complexity and ingenuity of design, until, having started with the hollowed-out canoe, we end with the 'Queen Mary'. It seems to be a glorious saga of human endeavour. But was it really like this? Was this development as inevitable as it appears? Supposing James Watt had not discovered the steam engine, or Darby of Coalbrookdale had not found out how to smelt iron with coal, the story of the ship would have been radically different. Human 'progress' is, in reality, more a matter of chance and effort, of stumbling on with no clear end in sight.

Then there is another point. 'Line of development' history needs not less detailed knowledge than other ways of working, but more, though this might not appear so at first sight. To illustrate this, let us take another study that is frequently carried out in schools, that of clothes. This at first seems deceptively easy to undertake. The children simply work through costume, happily drawing ladies in pointed mediaeval hats, then in Elizabethan ruff and farthingale, then in crinoline, and finally in modern liberated clothing. But, in reality, the study of fashion is a highly complex and sophisticated matter. The influences on it are many and subtle, ranging from the production methods of the time to the respective roles of men and women at a given moment in society. To gain anything real from such a study, children need a depth of knowledge and a subtlety of approach that they patently do not possess.

Another disadvantage of 'line of development' history is that it can only be applied to certain subjects. These are materialistic. One can study ships, roads, homes and cars, but not religion or art. If one applies this method to an intellectual subject, one automatically distorts it. Take the story of writing. One would start with the clay tablets of ancient Sumer, then proceed to the hieroglyphs of Egypt, and through to the Arabic and Roman script. The class would make clay tablets, try writing with a quill, and so on. But there is so much more to writing than this. It is the means of communication and expression, the very vehicle of civilisation. But all this would be left out, for it could not be incorporated into this approach. What the class would really be studying is how writing is done.

Nevertheless the 'line of development' approach remains a valuable way of teaching history, provided it is used thoughtfully and with a clear realisation of its limitations. Many of its shortcomings can be overcome if background books, rich in information, are used at the same time. Children should be encouraged to develop an inquiring approach. They should not just accept the fact that the Elizabethan ship has sails, but should say to themselves 'Why was this so? And what happened if there was no wind? I'll find out.' Finally, the teacher should indicate by his or her attitude that the 'line of development' study undertaken at a particular moment is not the be-all and end-all of the matter; behind it lies all the richness of many-sided human experience.

There is a wealth of books for children of all ages to use in 'line of development' history, many of them beautifully produced. Most of the firms which produce reference books for children also publish outline accounts of special subjects: the Longman *Then and There* series is an example. An interesting point arises when some of the 'line of development' books are compared to some of the 'patch' books. Take, for example, Bancroft's exciting study of pirates. It is the story of pirates from the earliest robbers who sailed the seas, right up to the modern hi-jacker. But is this book a study in depth of a number of pirates, or is it about the history of piracy? Is it a series of 'patch' studies, or is it a 'line of development'? It is hard to decide, and the same is true of many of these books. The answer really depends on whether the subject has enough inner coherence, or logical development through time, to merit being seen as a 'line of development'. It is an interesting reflection on the nature of history.

The most common 'line of development' studies made in schools are those tracing the history of towns, villages and transport. One does not have to look far for books on these subjects. Some of the most beautifully illustrated are the Batsford books. However, there are many more unusual themes awaiting exploration, and it is a pity not to be venturesome. There is, for example, a book on *Man and the Atom* by J. Kennett (Blackie), which is a history of the atom and its discovery from Greek to modern times—surely very relevant to the present day. As well as the *Book of Pirates* Bancroft produce *The Book of Spies*. A study of piracy or spying through the ages would prove wildly popular with most children. Or what about the cinema? *Exploring the Cinema*, by K. Allen (Odhams), tells the story of film-making from the magic lantern to the present day. It actually explains how those great favourites of children, *Thunderbirds* and *Bugs Bunny*, are made and how the puppets work.

For rather older children, quite detailed books are published on such subjects as the development of surgery, parliamentary reform and public health. Macmillan and Penguin both produce a series of this kind. Slower school leavers might well be interested in books like those in the series *Topics Through Time* by G. and J. Kent (University of London Press), each of which traces the history of a single trade or occupation, such as the housewife, farmer, inventor, or builder. As with 'patch' history, one does not have to confine oneself to the written work in the 'line of development' study. Picture series and work-kits can be very useful.

If one likes the 'line of development' way of working, one can find text-books which cover a complete history course in this way. One of the best books of this kind is *The Lives of the People* by A. H. Hanson (Heinemann). Book II, for example, is an interesting account of the discovery of the world, dealing with not just geography, but also the discovery of the universe and the discovery of Man's ancestors. Book III of the same series covers the history of work and invention.

So far in this chapter we have discussed the kinds of book written for the history lesson, and how they may be used with children. When one thinks about it, a different historical philosophy underlies each approach. Perhaps we should end this chapter by considering how to teach children to use books properly, for, strangely enough, this is what many children do not know, and what they are never taught. This is another reason why so many interesting projects in the class-room fail, for how often does one see a child earnestly trying to digest an encyclopaedia, or copying out vast reams of a book he does not really understand?

One should always make sure, before children begin any historical study, that they know how to use a book. After all, the book is the form in which civilised men have, since the beginning of civilisation, transmitted information and ideas. It has a long history itself. The lay-out that we have adopted for books in our civilisation, the way each has chapter headings, and an index, is a matter of technicality, of historical accident, and this should be explained to children. Sumerian books and Roman books were quite different from ours, and the Chinese read from the back of the book and from the right to left, a fact that is comforting to the left-handed child, who often instinctively wants to do likewise. Learning how to use a book correctly is a matter of technique and practice, and it should be taught as such. In particular, children need to have the index explained to them, and they need to know the alphabet in order to use it properly. Once they have learnt to find their way around books, they will use them intelligently.

Perhaps the very first 'line of development' study one should carry out with a class is that of the book itself.

Closely allied to the question of the approach to be used in the history lesson is the question of the syllabus. Various superficial considerations at once spring to mind. A teacher must, for example, take into consideration the location of the school if he or she wishes to teach local history; he may wish to take into account what is being taught in other subjects so that his history teaching takes on a wider significance. Beneath these considerations, however, lie issues of a deeper importance, for they spring from the nature of history itself. Are there 'types' of history that are best suited to certain 'types' of children? I was once told that social and economic history was for the dull children and political history was for the bright ones. I have been puzzling over this ever since. Are certain periods in history more attractive, or easier for children in certain age-groups? Must history always be taught chronologically? These are the kind of questions teachers ask themselves when confronted with the task of drawing up a syllabus.

Perhaps we could take the last question first. Historical events do take place in time and it therefore seems obvious that a history syllabus must be ordered chronologically. It would not make sense, for example, to start children on the Tudors, proceed to the Ancient Greeks and finish up with Victorian England. Even to this, though, there can be exceptions, for it is feasible that it might make intellectual sense to follow a study of the nineteenth century scientists with a study of the discoveries of the Ancient Greeks.

I think that all these questions can be answered by considering the really fundamental one which underlies them, and this is why it is necessary to have a history syllabus at all. The first reason concerns the matter of choice. We cannot teach the whole of history because there is too much of it, so we have to choose what is to go in, and leave a whole lot out. The second reason why we have to have a syllabus arises from consideration of the nature of the children we teach, and this seems to me all important. We should have, at the back of our minds, some idea of a child's progress, or his mental development, and this enables us to put all the other problems into perspective. Any syllabus should bear in mind the nature of the children it is designed for and the stages through which their thinking will inevitably pass. One cannot be more specific than this, for the actual context of what is taught must depend on the individual teacher, his interests and skills, and on those of the children he is teaching. There is no reason why political history should not be taught to less able children, or why the sixth-form should not enjoy learning about the Stone Age as much as eleven-year-olds to whom it is usually taught. The important thing is that their teacher should have considered the material in relation to their needs and should have worked out the best approaches accordingly.

The really good syllabus should be so designed as to bring about a creative teaching situation.

3
The Creative Approach in the Teaching of History

I am aware that the word 'creative' has a broad meaning, but in this chapter I wish to confine its meaning to creative practical work. The handling of materials is basic to the development of intelligence. This needs to be said again and again. Long before a child learns to speak, it is building up concepts vital to its mental development. It comes to grasp such concepts as height, breadth, weight, texture and many more complex matters, long before it can put them into words. What is important to the child is not just the physical characteristics of the material world in which he lives, but the richness of their relationship to each other, and the emotional significance they come to acquire, which become sources of continual inspiration to the imagination and the intellect. Research has shown that there is a direct relationship between the environment of a young child and its intelligence in later life. The richer the environment in terms of the handling of materials and the opportunity to experiment, the higher the intelligence quotient is likely to be. Long after a child has learnt to speak, its handling of materials constantly enriches and stimulates its mind, stimulating it to form new associations and ideas. The same process continues throughout life, although it is vital in the early years. Perhaps this explains the joy with which grown-ups paddle in the sea on a sunny day, and the comfort they seem to derive as, transformed and peaceful, they let the sand trickle through their fingers.

It goes without saying that all these opportunities should exist for every child, and that every subject taught in school should offer them. This need is basic to education, whether the subject is history, geography, science or mathematics. Many teachers know from sad experience what happens to a child when this is denied. An increasing number of children come from homes where they must make no noise because of neighbours, can make no mess because their homes are so overcrowded, and can rarely go out because they live high up in flats and the streets are too dangerous. These children become silent, dull and apathetic. Many have never even seen a pair of scissors by the time they come to school. Somehow, the schools must make this up to them. By doing so, it is no exaggeration to say that we could make a vital contribution to the intelligence of our community.

There certainly seems to be a striking relationship between creative work and the development of verbal ability. It is as if creative work enables a child to reach forward intellectually. How such a change can be explained in terms of theory I am not sure, but I, and many teachers like me, have often seen a striking improvement in a child's written work following a practical session.

Often, also, one sees a marked improvement in a child's personality and self-confidence. Having completed a piece of work of this kind, a child seems more integrated and self-controlled. This kind of work can almost be said to have a therapeutic effect, and many a child's behaviour improves as a result of it. I think the reasons for this are fairly clear. The well-integrated person, child or adult, is the one who is in control of his own environment and of himself. Handling materials teaches this. It certainly teaches self-control for, as one cannot bully a piece of wood or lose one's temper with a piece of cardboard, one has to come to terms with them. One is also forced to face up to one's own mistakes. Words can cover up many a piece of muddled thinking, but materials never. A badly sawn piece of wood simply does not fit. The really good thing about this kind of work is that the child is working with his whole personality. His desire to achieve his piece of work gives him the strength to overcome his own weaknesses. It is a self-directed activity, and that is why it helps him.

Still, to many people, practical activity appears to have little relevance to an intellectual subject like history. I think this feeling is based on somewhat of a misunderstanding. People who think like this usually believe that intellectual qualities can only be expressed in words. This is not so. Indeed, in many ways, words are traps, and many an idea can be better expressed visually. Take but one example, the word 'village'. This word means something quite different when it is applied to Roman, mediaeval, eighteenth century or modern times. One would have to talk for hours on the subject in order to define the word accurately. But in a model, say, of a mediaeval village, there are all its characters portrayed to the eye—the three-field system, the common, the lord's manor, the bee-hives in the villagers' gardens, there is a picture of mediaeval life, more clearly portrayed than in any number of words.

One must also remember this, that in order to make the model a child has to undertake a considerable historical exercise. He has to find out a great deal of information before he can even begin. I have, many a time, been amazed at the very high standards children have in this respect. They have a far higher standard of accuracy when working by themselves than the teacher can ever impose.

One must emphasise, then, that creative practical work, though much else besides, represents also an intellectual exercise. The child may not even be able to put into words what he has learnt, but he has learnt it. These ways of working are very good ways of teaching history to small children, to backward children, or to those who find verbal expression difficult. It is characteristic of children between the ages of five and eleven that they think with their hands, so that this approach is very appropriate to them.

There are still other reasons why the creative approach has a lot to recommend it. It is a more natural, a more complete way of working, if you like, than many another method. The child is, after all, working with the whole of himself. Physically, he is able to stand up, kneel, move about, which is more natural to him than sitting at a desk. Mentally, he is using all his senses, eyes and hands, his sense of spatial relationships, he is solving problems all the time in his desire to be accurate. Emotionally, he is finding intense satisfaction in concentrating all his resources, overcoming any of his own deficiencies in the process, in making something creative. The joy with which children approach this work shows what it means to them. Perhaps the happiest sound a teacher can hear is the low buzz of activity, like the happy humming of bees, that pervades the classroom when children are working in this way.

Often, creative practical work entails the child working in a group, and this, too, is good for him. It is good for a group to pool its resources, using, say, Jill's aptitude for sewing, John's love of paint and Pat's ability to inspire others with his ideas. It is good for the individual child to learn to share the one pair of scissors, to borrow someone's needle and cotton and lend a rubber in return. These are lessons in social behaviour that we all have to learn. Here again, children are much stricter with one another than an adult would be with them. The lazy child, or the one destructive of other people's efforts, meets with short shrift from the rest of the group.

These, then, are some of the many reasons why the creative approach is important, one might say vital, to the teaching of history. Yet many teachers never attempt it. This is partly because they see it as simply a waste of time, 'just playing with paint and paper, instead of doing some real work', as one of them put it to me. The misconceptions underlying this attitude I have discussed already. More often, the reasons why this kind of work is not done in the classroom is that there are simply no facilities for it. Many—one would even guess the majority—of classrooms in this country are still crammed with rows and rows of desks facing the teacher, with unsuitable surfaces for practical work, with no water supply, and few facilities for storage and display. It seems a physical impossibility to do such work. Moreover, the teacher is often near exhaustion, and it seems much easier to deliver an oral lesson than to undertake the effort of collecting materials, organising the work and finally displaying it. It is still more tempting never to embark on such work if the class is rowdy and undisciplined, for, in the presence of paint and clay, the opportunities for bad behaviour are infinite. In fact, this kind of work represents a searching test for the teacher, and of her relationship with the children she teaches. If the relationship is a poor one, the whole thing will break down. Neither can this work ever be given to children as an escape from the ordeal of oral teaching, or as a refuge from the class. Every teacher knows that the success of any way of teaching depends, to a large extent, on a good relationship with the class. If this breaks down, no method, however attractive in itself, will succeed.

There is another, more subtle reason why many teachers dislike practical activity in the classroom. It springs from a broad difference between the mind of the adult and that of the child. The adult dislikes 'mess', the child loves it. The adult has perfected more abstract ways of controlling his world, but the child, particularly the young one, still relies on his hands and senses as interpreters. To the adult, who has long ago cast away such childish things, the apparent messiness of children is seen, not merely as distasteful, but as an implicit threat to his own orderliness. His instinct therefore is to suppress it. This is what lies behind the deep reluctance of many teachers to allow practical work, and it certainly explains the near contempt with which many of them view it.

Of the various difficulties in this approach to history teaching, the practical ones are probably the most potent. Yet these can be overcome to a great extent. In the following pages I suggest various ways of working in the classroom, and there are many things it is possible for children to do even in restricted conditions. These are only suggestions, things I have seen done or done myself, and once you have embarked on this kind of work ideas will flood into your mind.

The first essential is to have plenty of materials ready before actually beginning. The point is to provide each child with the richest selection of materials possible—textures, colours, shapes and sizes—and it is a good idea for the class to start collecting well before hand. If you keep big cardboard boxes permanently in a corner in a classroom, everybody can put into them anything of interest they find. One box can be used for materials, another for wool, another just for anything interesting, like an egg-box or an empty tea packet that has caught someone's eye. It is worth keeping separately specially useful things, like circular shapes that can be used as wheels, cylindrical shapes that can be used for funnels and chimneys, cellophane for windows and water and materials that can be used for making people's faces and hair. Everyone in the class can add things to the boxes as they find them; by encouraging children to do this, you will be stimulating them to be aware of the things they see around them every day. Just before they begin the actual piece of work it is a good idea to take them out for a walk and let them pick up stones and twigs, many of which have fascinating shapes.

More than anything else, children of all ages love to make the people of the past. There are many ways of doing this. The simplest way is to let the children draw and cut out the shapes from card, or even paper, and then dress them. The figures can be painted and dressed with material, with wool for hair; they can even be embroidered with simple stitches. Once made, these paper and cardbord people can be hung in a frieze on the wall or can, much to the amusement of the class, be mounted on a roundabout.

A popular and easy way of making historical people is to make bottle dolls. Some of these are illustrated opposite. These are made from the plastic containers in which detergents and cosmetics are sold. It is wise never to use glass bottles or those which have contained strong chemicals. It is also wise to clip the tops off the plastic bottles before allowing them to be used, for they make very good water pistols!

A bottle bears a marked resemblance to the human shape. With head and arms (made from stuffed nylon stockings) added, or even with just an old tennis ball for a face, it can be dressed and made into a person. Small and backward children, as well as older ones, love to make these bottle dolls, for they are easy to handle. There is one golden rule in this kind of work—the smaller and less able the child, the *bigger* the object should be. The small child needs a big object, a needle with a big eye so that it is easy to thread; the older child can, and often loves to, make tiny objects with intricate decoration.

Smaller figures can be made of pipe-cleaners, which can be bought from any tobacconist. For a person about six inches high you need three pipe-cleaners. Twist them as shown in the diagrams to form a kind of skeleton. Then wind wool, or thin strips of material, tightly round the skeleton, shaping the figure as desired. When the shaping has been completed, a needle and cotton run up and down it will help it keep in place. The figure can then be dressed.

Bottle dolls

Pipe-cleaner figures

These little people can be bent into various attitudes, and are useful for peopling houses and castles. There is one slight difficulty, and that is that the men will not stand up by themselves. The women will, due to their

Mediaeval people, made from pipe-cleaners

Figures made from papier-mache and rolled paper

full skirts. The solution is to make bases for the men to stand on, from Plasticine, playdough, or wood. Some of these figures can be seen in the photograph opposite.

Papier-mache figures can be very effective; the photograph above shows a papier-mache Victorian boy in a sailor suit made of tissue, and with a tissue-covered face; an Anglo-Saxon peasant (papier-mache head, stuffed body and pipe-cleaner hands); and on the right a fine lady made entirely of rolled paper and light card.

Bigger figures, varying from one to eight feet tall, can be made from

Edwardian lady, made from chicken wire

galvanised wire netting. An Edwardian doll made in this way can be seen above. Wire netting can be bought from any hardware shop. Cut a roll of netting with wire cutters for the body and head, and shape it by squeezing it with your hands. (Wear gloves if your hands are tender.) Then attach separate rolls of netting for the arms and feet, as shown in the diagrams opposite. They can be tied on.

The roll of netting may need weighting with stones or clay if it is very tall, in order to keep it upright. Then it can be dressed. The face can be made in various ways. A simple way is to stuff a nylon stocking and crayon or sew on

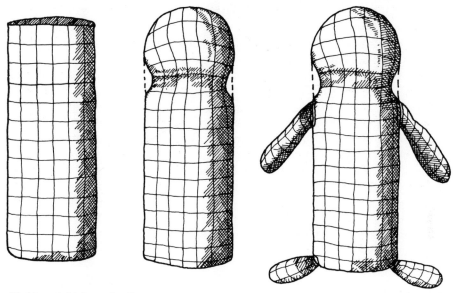

Making a chicken wire figure

the features. A more sophisticated way, which older children will enjoy, is to spread a thin layer of Plasticine over the face area and model the nose and mouth and eyes. Paste strips of tissue paper with Polycell or flour paste, and paste one layer of strips across the modelled clay, and one layer lengthwise, as shown below. Allow this to dry for about a day, and then the face is ready

Making the basic head: 1 Face is covered with Plasticine and modelled. 2 Strips of paper are placed lengthwise. 3 Strips of paper are placed crosswise and left to dry

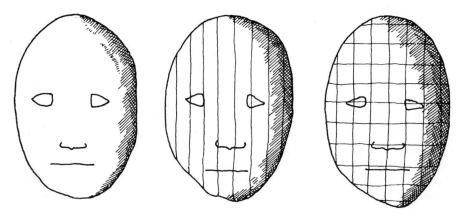

for painting with poster paints. The features of the Edwardian lady were made in this way.

A group of children would thoroughly enjoy making a life-size knight in armour and his lady using these materials.

Another very popular way of working is to allow the class to make historical masks. These are even more popular if they are made in such a way as to allow the children to wear them: that is, with holes for breathing and seeing through. The easiest way is to use balloons. Every child starts with a blown-up balloon, small size. (If you intend to blow them all up yourself it would be well to buy a balloon pump from Woolworth's.) The first step is to draw a face in pencil on the surface of the balloon. Then stick strips of sticky newspaper lengthwise and across, modelling the features as you go. Allow the face to dry, and paint it. Then comes the exciting bit: pop the balloon, remove the shreds of rubber, and there is the mask, all ready for the finishing touches of hair, helmet, moustache and so on. The stages in making this kind of mask are shown below.

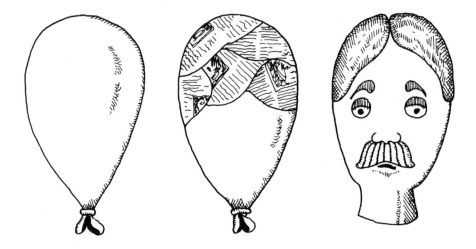

Balloon mask: 1 The balloon is blown up. 2 Sticky paper is placed over it and modelled. 3 The balloon is popped and the mask is painted

A mask that fits the individual face more closely can be made in the following way. You need galvanised wire, both medium and thin, and wire cutters. First make a halo of medium wire to go round the head for which the mask is intended. Then make a chin strap which is attached to the halo, and then 'spectacles'; join the three together, keeping the wire points made by the joins pointing outwards. These steps are illustrated in the diagram opposite. You now have the three dimensions of the head. The next step is to remove the framework from the head and make a netting over the frame, using the thinner wire. Cover this wire network with layers of sticky paper, and leave it to dry for a day or two, when it can be painted and decorated. These stages are shown below. If you wish to preserve the mask indefinitely, coat it with clear varnish, obtainable from Woolworth's or any paint shop. The results can be very striking. The best masks I have seen were a splendid Viking chieftain, whose fiercely be-whiskered face stared down at us from a wall for a whole term, and the face of Rameses II, a famous pharaoh, whose slanting eyes and half smile reminded us of the sunshine of Ancient Egypt throughout a dull and dreary winter.

These are just two simple ways of making masks. They can also be made in other ways—by first modelling a clay base, for example, covering it thickly with Vaseline, and sticking layers of pasted paper over that. When the clay dries, the mask can be lifted off.

Children love to make these models, for nothing brings the past alive so vividly as to create with your own hands the people who lived in it. Much of this work can be done in ordinary classrooms.

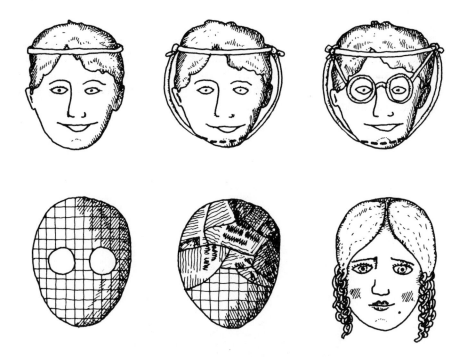

Wire framework for a mask: 1 The halo. 2 Chin-strap is added. 3 'Spectacles' are added. 4 The framework is covered with fine netting. 5 The netting is covered with sticky paper and modelled. 6 The paper is allowed to dry and the mask is painted

If the children create, not only the people of the past, but also the scenes against which these people lived and worked, then their picture will be even fuller. These models need not be intricate affairs. Many can be two-dimensional. It is easy to make a collage picture, for example, glueing and sewing material, dried grasses and flowers as well as using paint. Figures can be lightly stuffed with cotton wool or nylon to make them stand out. The most colourful example from my own experience was a huge collage picture of the sea in Cambrian times, made by a class of backward eleven-year-olds. As no one knows for sure what these early forms of life looked like, these children could give free rein to their imagination. Everybody brought something—buttons, odd beads, coloured paper—everything went in. They created a most vivid scene, and one which stayed in their minds for a long time, I know, for they often referred to it.

Children can also make three-dimensional models of the towns and villages of long ago, or of a great event, such as the Armada. These, though a bigger undertaking than a picture or a model of one person, do not have to be huge, and many can be made at a child's own desk. Supposing each child has made some pipe-cleaner figures of, say, Victorian people. A background for these can be made from three pieces of cardboard stuck together so that the right and left sides bend round to form a room, as shown below.

These 'walls' can be painted and decorated in a manner typical of the time, and the furniture made of matchboxes and cardboard. One could build up a picture of all the rooms in a Victorian house in this manner, and the models can easily be laid flat and stored when not in use. Alternatively, empty shoe boxes and cardboard boxes can be turned into rooms.

Making a background

There will be times when you want groups of children to make much larger models. This work is thoroughly enjoyable, but, being a larger undertaking, needs careful organising. It is important, not only to have all the materials ready, but also to let the children understand clearly what they have to do. In particular, they need to be set a clear time limit. If a class has a formal time-table, it may well be spending two periods a week on history. In this case, it will need at least three weeks to complete a model. If one has a freer arrangement of time, it is, of course, much easier. In any case, it should be made clear by when everything is to be finished, for nothing is more depressing than a piece of work that drags on and on, so that some groups have finished and some groups have not, and everybody loses interest.

This kind of work presents an excellent opportunity for children to work in groups. They should be allowed to choose the people they are going to work with, and they usually settle this quickly, forming themselves into groups of from four to six. Having seen that all are settled, and having provided items like scissors, glue, needles and cotton, the teacher should recede quietly into the background, making herself available for advice when asked for. The children will do the rest, making the overall plan and allotting individual tasks with a speed, efficiency and discipline that a teacher can rarely surpass. One can learn a very great deal about the children one is teaching by quietly watching them at this work.

There are several ways of making three-dimensional models, ranging from the very simple to those that will last almost indefinitely. For all models a base is needed—say four feet by three of hardboard or fibreboard. These bases can be used again and again. For buildings, cardboard boxes can be used, glued where necessary or stuck with sticky paper, then painted with poster paints. The people can be made in any one of the ways already described in this chapter; trees and scenery can be made from the various materials one has been storing. Children never have any difficulty in finding ways to make things.

A more permanent layout for a model can be made in the following way. Build up a ground-work on the base, using cardboard boxes, tins, wads of material and so on, to give the contours desired. Secure this material on to the base by sticking it down with Sellotape. The diagram below shows this stage.

Layout for a model : building up the ground work – material is secured to the base with Sellotape

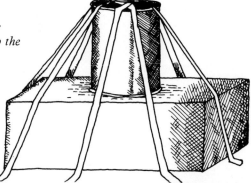

This gives your model its basic contours. Then stir Polyfilla, Polycell or potter's plaster, which can be bought at any hardware shop, in a tin or plastic bowl (because it is easy to clean) of water until it is of the consistency of thick batter. The next stage is to soak thin strips of gauze, thin material, or newspaper in the plaster solution. Leave them in the solution for about a minute, then take them out and cover the whole of the base and contours with these strips. If you have the right consistency of plaster, you should now be unable to see the weave of the material. The diagram below shows this stage.

Contours are covered with gauze and left to dry

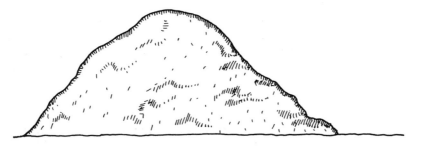

Then leave the whole model to dry for two days, when the plaster will be white and hard. It can then be painted with poster colours. If you give it a coat of clear varnish when the paint has dried, the model will last indefinitely. Houses, streams and people can then be added. This kind of modelling is also a good way of making a permanent layout for a model railway or racing track very cheaply, so that children can use this method to good purpose at home.

Scenery is painted and details added

One or two materials deserve mention for being useful in any kind of modelling. There is always Plasticine; Aloplast is a similar material. You can also make your own play-dough very cheaply. Mix 2 lb of flour with 1 lb of salt and add water until it is the consistence of clay. This material can be moulded, allowed to set, painted and varnished. A new material has recently appeared on the market which has all the advantages of clay and which dries hard in hours without firing. Originally from Italy, it is called Das. It can be modelled, painted with poster-paint or tempera, and varnished with Varni-Das to give a vitreous, ceramic-like finish without the necessity of using a kiln. It is available in most large stores or stationers, or a list of distributors can be obtained from Wiggins Teape (Stationery) Ltd (for address, see page 154).

Handwork need not be confined to the classroom. Various kinds, valuable in the teaching of history, can be carried on out of school. Taking brass rubbings in churches is an increasingly popular activity. Permission must first be obtained from the vicar, and he may both charge a small fee and restrict the number of rubbings taken, as many brases are being literally rubbed away. Each child needs a roll of white paper—ceiling paper will do—a stick of heel-ball from a cobbler, a clean duster, a soft nailbrush, and some weights. The paper is unrolled over the brass figure, perhaps a mediaeval knight, and weighted down at the corners. It is then rubbed all over with the nailbrush so that the outline shows through. Finally it is rubbed evenly all over with the flat of the heel-ball, so that the effigy is revealed. This is your brass rubbing. Sprayed with fixative, it will keep indefinitely; in fact, brass rubbings have become very popular as wall hangings in homes.

Having discussed some of the ways in which the creative approach can contribute to the teaching of history, I would like now to take up a point which often troubles teachers. How can this kind of work be judged? How does one know what it has given the children, if anything at all? It is tempting to adopt the kind of criteria one might use for other work, such as the degree of accuracy, whether it is 'good' enough to be put out for Open Day, how much factual information has been learnt and can be verbally recalled, and so on. It is true that when one studies the models the children have made, such as those reproduced in the photographs in this book, one can see a great deal of historical knowledge, but other things matter equally. The reason for encouraging children to do this kind of creative work is to give them the richest possible experience from it, and this experience can only relate to their own individual needs and personalities. Imagine two children. One is Joan, bright, good with her hands, who can toss off quite a sophisticated piece of work with comparatively little effort. The other is John, big, fumbling and awkward, for whom any kind of manipulation means a tremendous effort. John's piece of work will probably stand for far more in terms of endeavour and lessons learnt than Joan's, which will doubtless look the more attractive. In fact, by this kind of inner standard, John should have 'A' and Joan 'E', if marks we must have. Once I taught a little girl of eight who did nothing

Two bottle dolls and a figure made from sticks and paper

with her piece of clay but mould and handle it. She 'made' nothing, but the experience was valuable to her because her pleasure and excitement showed that she had discovered a new medium. Again, children who have been deprived of working with materials will at first produce work that is poor by any objective standards, yet they are the very ones who need the experience most.

There is another point to remember, which is that children see things differently from adults. This has already been discussed in the first chapter. What is significant to children is not necesarily so to an adult. Look at some of the models of people reproduced above: the mediaeval king, for example. His crown is out of all proportion to the rest of him. However, what might appear to be an inaccuracy may well represent a flash of insight, for the crown, to the child, is the very symbol of kingship. One often sees this kind of perspective in children's models, as one does in their drawings.

The real benefit to children from this kind of creative work will be largely unseen and will have no outward manifestation, for it relates largely to themselves. The good teacher, however, one who is sensitive to her class and to the individuals in it, will understand instinctively its importance. Not only is it a valuable approach to the teaching of history for children of all ages, and of all kinds of ability, it is an intellectual and social discipline that goes beyond the bounds of any one subject.

All that I have said so far applies very much to younger children. As they grow older, children develop adult standards of knowledge and accuracy. Boys especially often develop a passion, from the age of about nine onwards, for building intricate models to scale—scenes such as the Battle of Waterloo, with all the soldiers laid out in exact formation, every detail of their uniforms correct. They are obsessed, not so much with self-expression as with absolute accuracy. Some will build working models of machinery, like Watt's steam engine. I knew a boy who made a cannon that he could actually fire the length of the classroom. This kind of modelling is obviously an excellent historical exercise. Several firms (Airfix is one) make sets of soldiers of past centuries, which can be painted in exact detail and used for these scale models. Also very useful are the models of ships, cars and aeroplanes of the past that are made by the same companies. They can be bought in do-it-yourself kits from any toyshop or Woolworth's.

From the teacher's point of view, the real battle often begins when the children's work is finished. She may find herself in a cramped, crowded classroom, with lots of lovely work on hand and no way of displaying it. I should like therefore to end this chapter by saying a few words on making the best of a classroom, however inadequate.

Everyone should try to spend a few moments now and again appraising the classroom critically. It may well be cramped, but corners can often be used or, if there is a high ceiling, lines can be strung from wall to wall on which to hang pictures. There is usually one part of the room which forms a natural focal point, that part to which the eyes automatically swing as one comes through the door. This can be used in a special way. I once used a part of a wall like this by mounting 'A Changing Picture' on it. This was a history picture that I changed every day, before the children arrived. They would rush in to see it, intrigued and mystified as to how and why it changed. I refused to say, and although they were eleven, it never occurred to them that I had changed it myself. When I left, I took my secret with me. Ideally of course all the walls of a classroom should be suitable for display purposes by being covered with board.

When space is short, collapsible furniture that can be erected temporarily and then dismantled and stored is a great help. Square Tube Systems Ltd (for address, see page 154) make 'square-lock' furniture, which enables articles such as display units, tables and bookcases to be constructed by using different combinations of basic shapes. Alternatively, one can make one's own temporary shelves, using planks of wood and bricks as shown below.

Peg-board (hardboard with holes in it), purchased from any wood yard, is an invaluable display material in the classroom. M. Myers & Son Ltd (for address, see page 154) make a variety of metal fittings that fit into the holes and make it possible to display books, pictures and models.

Dull, dreary walls can be brightened in a variety of ways. The great thing is to be keenly aware of one's surroundings and the opportunities that exist in it, just as one would want the children to be. Many cheap, easily-obtainable materials make attractive backgrounds for display—materials such as corrugated paper, the vivid blue packing that one sees round apples and fruit in the greengrocers, odd lengths of wallpaper and pieces of material. If one lives near a market, much of this can be had free.

It is wise to keep certain equipment like lettering pens, glue and mounting paper on hand for display purposes. These, and many others, can be obtained from the Visual Aids Centre (for address, see page 154).

There are a few useful rules when it comes to displaying creative work in the classroom. One must always remember the purpose of the display. First and foremost, it is meant to be seen. Whatever is on display should be clearly seen from every other part of the room. So often one sees sheets and sheets of closely written file-paper pinned up on classroom walls, which no one ever reads, intrinsically good though the work may be. Lettering should be large. Another point worth remembering is that the eye-level of a child is much lower than that of an adult, so everything needs to be displayed that much lower. Adequate space should always be left between one picture or model and the next, for cramped work is always painful to the eye.

The classroom, with the children's work displayed around it, should be the home of a little community—gay, colourful and stimulating.

4
Original Sources and the Teaching of History

By original sources we mean anything that actually dates from the period of history concerned. What springs to mind first is contemporary writings: say 'original sources' to most people and they immediately think of a mass of old documents, written on parchment in almost indecipherable writing. However, other relics from the past are original sources. There are the utensils that people used, such as the pointed jars in which the Ancient Greeks stored their wine; there are the weapons, such as the flints with which early man fought for survival; and the tools, such as those that hammered out the iron machines of the Industrial Revolution. Buildings, too, are original sources; so are pictures, drawings and even people.

All these things have a unique quality in that they are the raw material of history. Every historian has to use them, and it follows that children cannot really understand the nature of history unless they, too, have this experience. The problem is, how can this be given them?

Ten years ago, original sources were rarely used in the history lesson, as they were considered far too difficult for children to handle. Recently, however, they have become increasingly popular. Partly this trend is the result of a desire to return to the grass-roots of the subject, to make history as concrete a subject as possible.

There is a strong feeling that the use of original sources makes history more real. Perhaps, also, we are seeing in this return to original material the results of a more child-centred education. Children today are much less inclined to accept the words of their elders. If you tell them that dinosaurs lived on earth long before Man, or that King John died of over-eating, they want to be told how we know. This spirit of enquiry is an excellent thing. It is the essence of historical research, and by introducing children to original material, we can at once answer their questions and begin to teach them what history is about.

Still, it does not occur to many people that original sources can be used while children are young. We are inclined to think of using them as a highly academic exercise, requiring considerable maturity. This is true of some sources in history, but not of all. In fact, children are at their most inquiring in their early years. It is at the infant and junior stage when they drive parents and teachers mad by their continual questions and desire to experiment. This is all part of the same strong drive—the desire to find out. Psychologically then children should be introduced to this primary material as early as possible, at any rate by the age of seven. Written sources will be beyond them, although they ought at least to have the opportunity of acquainting themselves with these; other forms of material they can use to some purpose.

There is one original source that we all possess, and carry around with us all our lives. It is our own name. What better way is there of introducing history to a small boy or girl than to explain the origin of his or her own name? Let us take first names, or Christian names, as they are commonly called, first. Many of these are thousands of years old, far older than surnames. They embody the respect ancient peoples had for certain virtues, their feeling for the beauty of nature, and the love they felt for their children. It is very satisfying to know that you carry a proud name, like a banner, through your life. How nice to know, if you are only six, that your name Roger means 'the famed spearman', or that you are Kenneth, 'the good-hearted' (Celtic). Gillian and Julia, both Lain names, mean 'soft-haired'; Jean, variants of which are found in countries throughout the world, means 'the gracious gift of God'. Sometimes names which people believe to be modern and trendy turn out to be extremely old. Take Wendy for instance, commonly thought to have come into fashion for girls with Barrie's *Peter Pan*. It is actually a derivative of 'Wendelin', an old Anglo-Saxon name which has the charming meaning of 'the wanderer'. To explain to a class of young children the meaning of their own first names is an excellent and imaginative way of introducing them to history. I have never known anybody uninterested, and that applies to grown-ups too.

There are various books on first names. There is the *Gem Dictionary of First Names*, published by Collins, and sometimes the various women's magazines supply a great deal of free information.

This study of first names can be taken further, for they come from four main sources: from the Greek and Latin through to the French, Italian and Spanish languages; from the Teutonic through to the Germanic and Old English tongue; and from the Semitic, which is mainly Hebrew. When the names from these sources are grouped, they give a clear picture of these ancient peoples. Take, for example, the Hebrew names Elizabeth meaning 'to the Lord I consecrate thee'; Simon, 'the obedient'; and Abigail meaning 'a father's joy'. Surely these names embody the devout religious fervour and pride of family that characterise the Hebrew people even to this day. In contrast, the Greek names Daphne, 'the maiden'; Margaret, 'the pearl'; Alexander, 'the defender of men'; and Philip, 'lover of horses', could only have come from a people who at once loved nature and were great fighters. The Saxons too loved nature and respected the man of battle, but the subtle difference in their attitude comes through unmistakably in the names they gave their children. There is Albert, 'he of noble descent'; Gerald, 'masterful with the spear'; and then the delightful Ella, 'the friend of the elves' and Mervin, 'friend of the sea'. The Saxons seem to have felt a personal involvement with nature, compared to the more aesthetic, abstract feeling of the Greeks. The wandering Celts put poetry into the names they gave their children. There is Douglas, 'the dark stream'; Meredith, 'the protector of the sea'; and the charming Cymbeline, 'the lady of the sun'. If one collected and grouped the names of all the children in one's class, one would have much first-hand information about our forbears. It could even lead to a study of their achievements in the world.

Surnames have a much shorter history than first names, but in many ways they are even more interesting, for they provide an apt commentary on the way in which our society has evolved. Only when society became complicated, by increasing population on one hand and the growth of specialised occupations on the other, did surnames become necessary. Or perhaps there were too many people of the same first name, so that 'Hugh the Smith' had to be distinguished from 'Hugh the Carpenter'. Surnames tell us about a person's ancestors. If you have a Smith, a Miller, or a Carpenter in your class, you can be sure of some distant forbears' way of earning a living. These very common names are a commentary on the economic life of mediaeval times. On the other hand, John Bigg undoubtedly had tall people in his family (and very likely still has, heredity being what it is), while Lucy Bridgeman's ancestors once lived by a bridge. Sometimes, amusingly, a surname denotes a physical quirk or characteristic of one's ancestors that caught the fancy of his neighbours. Such must have been the case with 'Cruikshank', 'crooked leg'. Some names, of course, owe their origin to the frailties of human nature, for they are now mis-spellings, and date from an occasion when an almost illiterate ancestor tried to write his name, and wrote it wrongly.

To gather up the names of the children in one's class is to gather up living history. Their names are vital proof that the children are, indeed, part of the past they are learning about. The study of names has grown popular in recent years, and simple, interesting books for the layman are available such as *Your Book of Surnames* by J. P. Hughes (Faber), or *The Penguin Dictionary of Surnames* by B. Cottle. Closely allied to the name as an original source is the heraldic device. Heraldry is really a picture language, originating on the battle-fields of many years ago, when few men could read and uniform was not worn, so that the picture on shield or banner was a way of distinguishing friends from enemies, as well as acting as a rallying point. The brilliant colours of the heraldic device and its often romantic origin make it an attractive study for children. At one time heraldry was a field for the experts, but recently books have been written on it that appeal to the average reader. Two I know, *The Observer's Book of Heraldry* by C. R. Mackinnon (Warne) and *Discovering Heraldry* by R. H. and S. Wilmott (University of London Press Ltd), can be read and enjoyed by children.

Our names and heraldic devices (if we are aristocratic enough to possess the latter) are original sources that we carry with us. Others, equally vivid and suitable for use with young children, are living people. Strangely, their value in the history lesson is almost completely overlooked. This is partly because we see the world in an adult perspective, forgetting that, to a child between seven and fifteen, even someone of thirty can remember what to him is the distant past. A group of teachers from an average school could, between them, give a fascinating picture of, say, twenty years ago. Suppose one gathered together a group of people who lived through the Second World War and let them talk about it. I was one myself, an evacuee. My memories are of homesickness in the beautiful countryside, of listening to the German bombers throbbing on their way to London, my home, of being caught in an air-raid during a holiday and watching my own school burn down. I still have my old ration book and identity card. However, my brother (and I think I could persuade him to come and talk to my class, and to bring his old uniform) had quite a different experience, for he was a torpedo pilot in the Fleet Air Arm. He travelled all over the world, and his life seemed to alternate between having a roaring good time and facing great danger. One of my friends, on the other hand, was hardly affected at all by the war. She lived in the depths of the country, far from the conflict. As her father kept a farm, rationing did not bother her family. If we all told the children about our experiences, we would face them with some of the problems of making history. What is the truth about the Second World War? Why do our accounts all differ? Can one trust everybody's opinion to the same extent? Several witnesses were only children at the time; might they not remember inaccurately? Lastly, is it possible to construct a picture of this period in history from what these witnesses say, or is something lacking? Merely by discussing these and other questions with children, one is introducing them to the joys and problems of handling original sources, of making real history. Teachers are often shy of asking people outside school to come in and talk to children, but I can truthfully say that I have found them invariably willing, even eager, to come.

If real people are unobtainable, one can at least produce some of the objects that personalise their lives—photographs, old clothes, some letters, perhaps. Better still, one can sometimes tape-record their memories. Certainly one could build up a varied collection of tape-recordings of this century. There are people alive today who can remember both wars, the Slump, the coming of television, as well as many personalities. I once tape-recorded for a class the memories of a very old lady, who wore clogs when she worked in a Lancashire cotton mill at the turn of the century. I also recorded the voice of a gallant old gentleman who emigrated to Canada before the First World War and lived as a cowboy near the Rockies. It is surprising what rich sources of history one's friends and family can be, and what an unexpected light they often throw on seemingly commonplace events.

There is considerable scope, and much fun to be had, in building up one's own collection of tape-recordings, and one can combine this with the classics now being produced by some of the publishing firms. As will be mentioned in the chapter on audio-visual aids, Longman are producing eye-witness accounts of great events in the twentieth century in the recordings to accompany their *Modern Times* series, and Decca (see page 153) has recorded excerpts from some of the speeches of Winston Churchill.

Pictures are also original sources, and are valuable for using with children who, for some reason, cannot handle language easily. Some are those actually created in and surviving from the past, like the illuminated manuscripts of the Middle Ages, while others are reproductions of historical objects, such as means of transport, cooking utensils, or tools. There is, also, nowadays, the kind of composite picture specially produced for the history lesson. While these are not original sources in the strict sense, many of their features are reproduced from objects that actually existed in the past, so that they can fairly be included in this chapter. Take, for example, a picture (from Macmillan's *History Picture Books* 5A, say) of a middle-class Victorian family at home. It is obviously an accurate representation of their dress, appearance and furnishings. All three kinds of picture can be used in the history lesson.

One of the best ways of reproducing the true pictorial source for the classroom is through the film-strip. A valuable series is produced by Educational Productions Ltd (see page 152), which offers subjects like *Mediaeval Sports and Pastimes* with illustrations taken from the borders of a fourteenth century Flemish manuscript. Other firms publish source books full of accurate drawings and photographs of historical objects. There are, for example, the *Picture Reference Books* published by the Brockhampton Press, and the *Picture Source Books for Social History* produced by Allen and Unwin. The museums also are gold-mines of pictorial source material, especially as their picture postcards have a high standard of accuracy and detail.

How, then, can pictorial sources best be used in the classroom? In some ways, they can be put to telling use, but in other respects they are limited in what they can achieve. It is worth while keeping clearly in mind the aim of using original sources, which is to bring the child into contact with first-hand historical material; this, in turn, helps him to develop a historical sense. The term 'historical sense' is in itself complex. It involves, firstly, the ability to see what is unique and specially appertaining to a certain period in time, then a critical ability involving the comparison of what is typical of one time with what is typical of another, and lastly the weighing of evidence and making of judgements about people and events. Pictorial sources can help a child towards some of these things, but not towards all. They can convey what is unique about an age very vividly indeed, but mainly with regard to the physical and the concrete. Take the German wood-cuts of the sixteenth century reproduced overleaf, showing the various trades of the time. They are taken from the *Picture Source Book for Social History, Sixteenth Century,*

101. Weaver

102. Smith

103. Hairdressers

104. Scissors grinder

Look for: scissors, woven basket, shampooing, towel drier, bandages (why?),
water dripping on to the grindstone (what for?). *These are German woodcuts, but are
true of Tudor England*

German wood-cuts of the sixteenth century: these can be found in the Picture Source
Book for Social History, Sixteenth Century *edited by Molly Harrison and
Margaret E. Bryant (Allen and Unwin). The original pictures are in the British
Museum.*

published by Allen and Unwin. These pictures show concrete objects—the scissors of the barber, the tools of the smith—they show the barber and the smith themselves, but not what they might be thinking. The religious conflicts of the sixteenth century were as much a part of it as the trades being carried on, but thoughts can only be expressed in words. Yet the German woodcuts do say something about the people of the sixteenth century, in some ways more subtly than an explanation in words could. It is amusing to see, in the picture of the barber's, the man in the right-hand corner having his hair firmly washed over a basin in much the same way as it is done today. The man in the barber's chair has much the same air of engrossed self-absorption as one can see any day in a modern High Street. But one would not see the barber's chair, or the interior of the shop or those men. It is not just the physical detail that is revealing, but the whole atmosphere of the picture. It is unmistakably sixteenth century. This wood-cut, then, does say something about the people, but it hints at them through material and physical detail. It does not give us enough.

It must be accepted then, that pictorial sources cannot say the ultimate about people. They are, however, very useful in helping a young child begin to develop a critical sense. Two pictures from Macmillan's *History Picture Books* 5A, 'Crowded Houses of the Industrial Age, 1850' (see page 62 of this book) and 'A Middleclass Family at Home, 1850s', portray aspects of life in Victorian England. When they are put side by side, they make a pertinent comment, the most obvious being the contrast between the rich and the poor in the nineteenth century. Each picture makes a statement, and when a child is presented with both he is encouraged to place one statement against the other; this is the essence of criticism. Or these pictures can be used in another way. Suppose the picture of the middle-class Victorian family is placed side by side with a picture from the same book, 'Wheat and the U-Boat Campaign, 1914–18'. How life has changed! The child looking at both pictures knows that clothes, machinery, and people's lives have altered through the century. He begins to feel a sense of development in history.

For a fuller and more sophisticated use of pictorial sources, they should be accompanied by verbal comment and explanation. Work-cards are an excellent way of stimulating children to make their own comment on what they see. Looking at the picture, 'Crowded Houses of the Industrial Age', one could ask on the work-card such questions as 'How did the people in the picture get their water?', 'Where did they keep their rubbish?', 'What musical instrument is the woman in the picture playing?' Some questions, such as the final one, the children may not be able to answer at once. This is all the better, for they will have to find out, either from you, or from carefully chosen reference books.

The skilful use of pictures means that original sources need not be confined to the older or more intelligent child. Used imaginatively, they are a valuable way of teaching history to the young, and even to the backward child.

Crowded houses of the industrial age, reproduced from History Picture Books 5 A, Victorian Times to World War I *(Macmillan) where it appears in colour*

What most people mean by an original source is the written original source. There are many written sources, comprising the books, letters, diaries, newspapers and translations of the past. The use of these sources, often in the form of facsimiles, has become more and more popular in the classroom in recent years. Apart from the general advantages discussed at the beginning of the chapter, the written source has certain qualities that the book written by the historian cannot possess, namely the qualities of vivid detail and emotional impact. There are obvious reasons for this. When a historian writes a book, probably many years after the events he is describing actually happened, his work inevitably gains in some respects and loses in others. He writes impartially, so that his work is objective. He is concerned with making valid generalisations about his subject, and this tends to take him away from the personal and intricate. He is involved with the nature of cause and effect in human events, and this gives his work a lengthy perspective not to be found in one person's individual viewpoint.

The contemporary written source is usually the complete opposite of all this. It is intensely personal, often partisan. It is written in the thick of some gripping event or dreadful experience, and therefore cannot possess the impartiality or the perspective that the passage of time brings. It is not in the least concerned with cause and effect in the broad sense of the term, for this can only emerge when events are not merely seen from a distance, but also correlated with each other. However, the written source possesses qualities that the written history has lost in its making. It makes tremendous impact on the reader, drawing him back into the past almost as if he were actually there; it possesses a wealth of vivid detail, often putting forward a tiny fact that makes the personality of a man or woman leap into life. It can make the reader feel actively involved.

This is what the Constable of the Tower of London wrote about Anne Boleyn, on the day of her execution in 1536—'She said, "Mr. Kingston, I hear I shall not die afore noon, and I am very sorry therefore, for I thought to be dead this time and past my pain." I told her it should be no pain, it was so little. And then she said, "I heard say the executioner was very good, and I have a little neck", and she put her hands about it, laughing heartily.' Through these few words speak the cruelty of Tudor times, and yet, too, the kindliness of one man who had seen many deaths but wished to spare his prisoner mental suffering. Through them also speaks the personality of Anne Boleyn.

The diaries of Pepys are famous and are usually quoted for his descriptions of the Fire and Plague in seventeenth-century London. But this is what he wrote about some music he heard at a play in 1668. He described it as 'so sweet that it ravished me, and did wrap up my soul so that it made me really sick'. In another passage, Pepys describes how he had his hair cut at the barber's and a boy played the violin while he was attended to. A historian might truly write, 'The seventeenth century was a musical age', but how much these two extracts from one man's personal journal add to this statement!

To go forward to the nineteenth century, a visiting Frenchman, M. Faire, described part of London in 1871 thus, 'On the stairs leading to the Thames they swam, more pale-faced, more deformed, more repulsive than the scum of Paris. Near them, leaning against the greasy walls, or inert on the steps, are men in astounding rags; it is impossible to imagine before seeing them how many layers of dirt an overcoat or a pair of trousers could hold; they dream or doze open-mouthed, their faces are begrimed, dull and sometimes streaked with red lines. . . . For a creature so wasted and jaded there is but one refuge—drunkenness.' Here, then, is the poverty of the nineteenth century, the other side to the might and splendour of Victorian England.

These extracts illustrate two of the ways in which the written original source can be used in the history lesson. It can be used illustratively, in order to illuminate a subject by its pertinent detail. It can also be used to recapture the spirit and atmosphere of a past age.

Most of this kind of material can be borrowed from the nearest public library. Sometimes these sources are not used so enterprisingly as they might be. Most teachers have heard of Pepys, but fewer use the diaries of his contemporary, Evelyn, and only rarely are children introduced to the less well-known journals of men like Marco Polo and Columbus.

Nowadays there exist specially compiled volumes of original documents for teachers to make use of in their classrooms. There is the popular *They Saw it Happen* series (Blackwell), four volumes of eye-witness accounts, ranging from late classical times to 1940, covering both Britain and Europe. On a more specialised topic, Macmillan have published *Sea Voyages of Exploration*, edited by G. A. Sambrook, which illuminates some of the world's great feats of exploration and discovery in the words of the men concerned. There is no shortage of original documents covering English history: there are J. S. Millward's two selections of documents from contemporary writings of the sixteenth and seventeenth centuries in England, and his volume (with H. P. A. Craft) on the eighteenth century (all Hutchinson), and Eyre and Spottiswoode produce twelve volumes of sources under the general title *English Historical Documents* (a thirteenth volume is in preparation).

The above publications are conventional sources of original material for use in the classroom. It is, however, fascinating and often amusing to work from less usual writings. Why not base some teaching on Mrs Beeton's cookery book, for instance, or on the *Railway Official's Directory* for 1922? Both are pertinent commentaries on their age. This kind of book can often be discovered in the lists of a firm specialising in works that are out of print. One such is S. R. Publishers Ltd, from whose list the two titles above are quoted. The same publisher is embarking on a new enterprise, that of reproducing rare manuscript material in micro-film. As it needs special equipment, micro-film cannot be used in many schools, but it may, in the future, provide a way of introducing older children especially to extracts from parish registers, newspapers and rare books that they might otherwise never see.

Recently, there has been a trend towards using written sources in the classroom in an entirely different way. They are used, not merely illustratively, but as a way of introducing the child to the technique of history. He is encouraged to understand the process by which the colourful, often prejudiced, eye-witness accounts, the catty comment on a political rival or colleague, the news-happy description of a journalist, becomes the balanced, measured judgement of the historian. Of course, this is the ultimate in history teaching and until recently it has always been considered too sophisticated a process for children to understand. But just because this is the ultimate in history teaching, it is important to introduce them to it as early as possible, albeit on a very simple level.

One can begin by presenting children with apparently conflicting views on a subject. Here, for example, are two opinions of Elizabeth Tudor. Both are taken from the 1485–1688 volume of *They Saw It Happen*. The first description was written by Sir John Hayward, a contemporary English historian. He writes, 'Her virtues were such as might suffice to make an Ethiopian beautiful, where, the more a man knows and understands, the more he shall admire and love. In life, she was most innocent, in desires moderate, in purpose just; of spirit, above credit and almost capacity of her sex, of divine wit . . . of eloquence; of wonderful knowledge both in learning and affairs' . . . and so it goes on.

Yet here is what André Hurault, the French ambassador in 1597, thought of Elizabeth. 'She is a haughty woman, falling easily into rebuke. In her own nature she is very avaricious and when some expense is necessary, her Counsellors must deceive her before embarking on it little by little. She thinks highly of herself and has little regard for her servants and Council . . . she mocks them.' He goes on to describe Elizabeth's dress, 'She kept the front of her dress open, and one could see the whole of her bosom, and often she would open the front of her robe with her hands as if she were too hot . . . Many of [her teeth] are missing, so that one cannot understand her easily when she speaks quickly.'

Why are these two accounts so different? Did both men know Elizabeth with the same degree of intimacy? Were they both equally honest? Or could it be that one man was English and the other was French, from a country with whom Elizabeth was not always on the best of terms? Coping with these questions might lead children to compare these sources of information with others, to arrive eventually at some conclusion, just as the historian does. At the very least, they would formulate some of the questions that have to be asked in the course of the historian's work.

The last few years have seen the emergence of study kits, or books of original sources in reproduced form, often photostated, for children to use themselves in the history lesson. This kind of presentation aims at making this kind of material easier for children to use. The reasons why this is necessary are clear. The historian, when he begins his work, already has a plan; he has considerable background knowledge of his subject; he has a shrewd idea of the questions he hopes to find answers for; he has a framework for his investigations. The child, when presented with original manuscripts in the classroom, has no such framework; he probably has very little historical background to the subject he is asked to study, and cannot unaided think of the right questions to ask. The study kits of original material have a two-fold aim: they reduce the problem of selection to a manageable scale for the child, by including only selected sources, and they shape the material so that it has more meaning for him. Usually this is done by grouping the manuscripts, drawings, maps and anything else that might be used, carefully round a given subject. The Essex Record Office Publications achieve this by offering such well-defined topics as *Law and Order in Essex* and *Highways and Byways of Essex*. The University of Newcastle publish an Archive Teaching Unit, among others on *Coals from Newcastle*, a study of the social and economic history of the north-east coalfield in the nineteenth century. Evans publish an interesting series called *History at Source*. One collection is entitled *Children, 1773–1890*, compiled by Robert Wood, who has also prepared *Law and Order, 1725–1886*; another is *Factory Life, 1774–1885*, compiled by Peter Shellard. Perhaps the most famous series of all is the *Jackdaws*, published by Jonathan Cape. Each envelope contains all kinds of original sources—there are reproductions of old maps, portraits, engravings and manuscripts. So far, there are over sixty titles. Sometimes the material in a study-kit is given coherence by being used in conjunction with another activity, like listening to a broadcast, or making a model. The B.B.C. recently produced study folders for their *History in Evidence* broadcasts, as well as pictures and reproductions of manuscripts. These have proved popular in the schools. The purpose of all these productions is the same; it is to make a mass of original material meaningful to a child.

Another promising new venture is on the way. This is a magazine called *Then*, published six times a year by Peter Way Ltd. Each issue takes one special year as its topic. If the year is 1901, for example, all the source material such as newspaper cuttings, extracts from magazines and so on, will centre on that year. The other years so far dealt with (early 1973) are 1848, 1920, 1745, and 1815. This is yet another approach to the use of original sources in the history lesson.

Nevertheless, the use of some of the folders in the classroom can prove to be a disappointing experience. It all seems such a wonderful idea, and one falls eagerly upon the gaily-coloured folders, only to collapse in confusion. How should a teacher faced with forty or more children use these folders? Should they be divided up among the class, or each child given one, or what? Can the children really get much out of such material without help? There are ways of helping children use these folders to the best advantage, and I should like to illustrate this by taking one of the Jackdaws, *The Slave Trade and its Abolition*. I do this in the full realisation that what is suitable and appealing for the children I have taught may not in the least be so for somebody else's, and also that only the individual teacher knows best how to adapt her ideas to the age-range and intelligence of her class. These are just suggestions. I am assuming that the children concerned are between the ages of seven and thirteen.

One opens *The Slave Trade and its Abolition* to find inside a list of contents and a mass of material. There are six broadsheets telling the story of slavery and how it was ended; there is an ink plan of a slaving ship as prepared by the Wilberforce committee to show how the luckless Africans were herded on board; a portrait of William Wilberforce; a bill advertising a slave auction in 1829; some selected pages from the journal of John Newton in his own handwriting describing the slave-trade; a remonstrance from the Council and Assembly of Jamaica to the House of Commons in 1789 protesting against proposed abolition; a sheet of statistics relating to the number of negroes delivered to the West Indies between the years 1689 to 1701; and a number of cartoons and pictures showing the life of the slave. Only a mature mind could make sense of this material unaided, but with help, quite young children can use it to advantage.

The first essential is to set aside anything that is unsuitable for the particular group of children one is teaching. The written sources in this folder are too difficult for really young children to understand. They can, however, get a lot from the pictures, and also the bill advertising the slave auction, particularly if these are discussed with them first. They might also like to read the journal of John Newton, although, as his handwriting is difficult to read, they should have the extracts typed out for them beforehand.

Before the children begin work on the folder they should know something of the background to the slave trade. Unless they have this, they will not be able to ask the right questions of the material they are working on. This background can be given by the teacher, or through appropriate reference books.

When they actually begin work on the documents themselves, all but the most able children need to be given some kind of framework into which to fit their research. The older, more mature child may know what he intends to find out, but the younger ones need work-cards. Suppose they are looking at the pictures on the large sheet entitled 'Sold into Slavery'. One can ask them on the work-card what is happening in the centre picture (a woman and her daughter are being auctioned); they can draw the branding irons which are reproduced; they can describe, from the drawings in front of them, how the slaves were marched across Africa to the trading stations. Or the children might be working from the bill advertising the slave auction. On it are listed the names of the actual slaves: two are only fourteen years old—might not some of the class imagine themselves to be one of these children and describe their sufferings? Used in this way, the material can be divided out among the class. It can also act as a starting point for further research, using simple reference books, or for stimulating activities like painting a picture or making a model.

Older children are able to use the written sources. Even these, though, are confusing if they are just handed out. I think it is helpful to classify the material, boldly and clearly, even further. The sources can be divided up according to subject matter and put into different, brightly coloured envelopes. The broadsheets could go into a red envelope (made by stapling sheets of paper together), with the words 'These tell you the story of slavery'. The pictures could be put into a yellow one, with the inscription 'These pictures tell you how the slaves were treated', and so on. Each coloured envelope could contain its own work-card.

The older, intelligent child can be handed the whole folder with no further classification, and asked to put together an account of slavery and the slave trade as an exercise in writing history.

These folders of original sources can give rise to various kinds of activity within the class. The contents can be used to make a display, and much learned in the process. Or they can be used as a basis for group-work. Groups can work on separate aspects of the slave trade, such as how it came about, the men who worked to abolish it, and what life was like on the Jamaican plantations. Each group could prepare an illustrated talk for the rest of the class.

The secret of using these folders seems to be to think out carefully beforehand exactly what one intends to do. The essentials to remember are that they cannot be used profitably unless the children have an adequate historical background, they must be given a shape that the child can handle, and they must give rise to activities appropriate to the age and abilities of the children concerned. There is one little problem that can easily be solved. Sometimes old manuscripts are difficult to read because the letters are formed differently from our own. Essex County Records Office produce sheets depicting the various ways in which our alphabet has been written as far back as the sixteenth century (reproduced opposite). With the aid of these, children might find it fun to try to decipher these old manuscripts, especially if they are equipped with a magnifying glass.

Some publishers are trying to solve the problems that surround the use of source materials in the classroom by placing selected documents in folders and adding assignment cards. An example is the *Exploring History* series, edited by A. Jamieson and published by Macmillan Education. This is an attempt to bring original sources within the reach of the average child, and each kit, on such topics as *Nelson's Navy, Houses and Homes, The Industrial Revolution, Transport*, and *Victorian Britain*, contains carefully selected facsimile documents, illustrations, and work cards.

Perhaps, though, we have become over-awed of late by the abundance of commercially-produced material for children. Many of these selections, whether in the form of study-kit, folder or book, are excellent, but there is nothing to stop the teacher from making her own. In fact, she has an advantage no editor producing material for children throughout the length and breadth of Britain can possibly have, for only she really knows her own pupils, and she can adjust the material accurately to their needs.

A student of mine recently made up a folder for a group of eight-year-olds she was teaching. Her subject was 'Family Life in Late-Victorian England'. She included a portrait of Queen Victoria; she made little models of Victorian people out of pipe-cleaners and dressed them beautifully to show their

A general alphabet of the old law hands (reproduced from Court-hand Restored, *by A. Wright, first published 1773)*

A general Alphabet of the Old Law Hands.

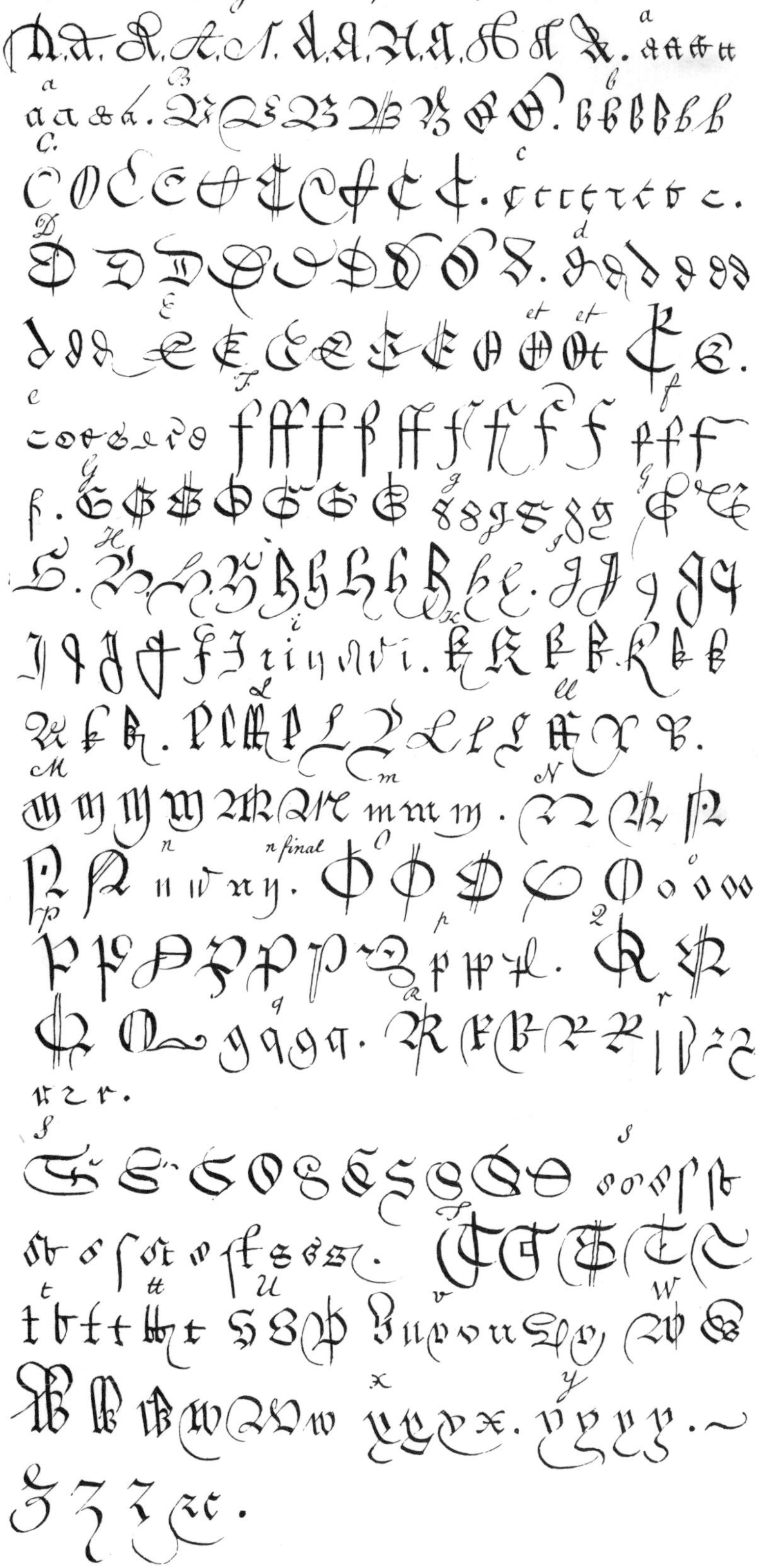

clothes; she put in pictures she had collected from various magazines to show what the family's furniture and house interior were like; she included a picture she had drawn herself of a table laden with food to show a typical dinner, and a tape-recording of music-hall songs as an example of how the Victorian liked to amuse himself. Lastly, most sensitively, I thought, she included a little bundle of materials and objects that the children could handle. There was a piece of very old lace, a button-hook, a thimble, and so on. Children love handling things. The materials covering each aspect of Victorian family life were enclosed separately, with a simple, clear explanation in few words, and the whole was enclosed in a brightly coloured folder. This was a most imaginative use of original material in the history lesson. Nobody is suggesting that any hard-worked teacher can produce forty such folders overnight, but the contents can be built up gradually. Older children often enjoy undertaking this kind of work for the younger ones, and learn a great deal in the process.

So far we have discussed in this chapter a variety of original sources and how each can be used in the history lesson. There are names, pictures and documents. There are also the objects of the past, like pottery, tools and even buildings that have come down to us through the ages. Archaeology is an increasingly popular hobby these days, and most people are aware that we possess many priceless treasures from the past. Some of these are so precious that they can only be seen in museums, but many teachers are unaware that certain local authorities and museums are prepared to lend out collections of materials to schools. The West Riding of Yorkshire has a collection of Roman pottery and household utensils that can be borrowed, together with an explanatory booklet. Surrey County Council also lends to schools. The Victoria and Albert Museum has collections specially prepared for children.

The value of such material in the classroom is that it has the quality of immediacy. To see a picture of a pair of Egyptian curling-tongs is one thing, actually to hold them in your hands, and perhaps to try them in your own hair, is quite another. It really does convince you that the Egyptian lady of fashion actually lived, and was as pernickety about her appearance as some of us are.

Nothing is nicer in the summer term, when the weather is good, than to take off with one's class on a day's outing to a historical site or a museum. Everyone intends to learn a lot of history. One can, however, be surprised, when the sandwiches have been eaten and the last picture postcard bought, at how little everyone has learnt. Perhaps this is to take a mean view of that great treat, the school visit. The value of such excursions goes far beyond the bounds of one's own subject, particularly in the case of children who live in deprived areas or who rarely go out of their own district. I remember going with a class of such children, ten-year-olds, to the Natural History Museum. The whole district turned out to see us go off; parents, aunts and younger brothers and sisters lined the streets as we marched along. When we got back and the children were asked what they remembered, nobody could remember anything, except one child who remembered all the railings. But at least we had been on the Tube, seen different people, found out a little more about the world.

More seriously, in so far as the teaching of history goes, the aim of taking children to see objects in a museum is exactly the same as it would be to show them these same objects in the classroom: it is to introduce them to material at first-hand, to convey to them that precious quality of immediacy. The trouble is that the trappings that surround such a visit, the excitement of going out of school, coupled with the way in which historical objects are often set out in a museum, all too often destroy this quality. Perhaps a few practical points should be borne in mind first. It pays to remember that an excursion of this kind can be physically exhausting, even for adults, and that children under the age of about seven are too young to make such an effort. Even when they are in the museum, the children will not be able to see everything, as there is too much, so that what you wish them to see should be carefully thought out beforehand. It should be remembered that most children cannot work steadily for more than about an hour at a time. Many museums have children's departments, with special children's lecturers, who are only too happy to help plan a class's work. One of the children's lecturers at the Natural History Museum and a colleague of mine recently planned a successful school visit like this: when the children arrived, they were given a short lecture and an hour's guided tour on the chosen subject, then a break. After this there was a finding-out session of another hour, using prepared work-sheets, then there was a long break for lunch in some nearby gardens. After lunch came a film, followed by half an hour in which the children could just wander around looking at anything that caught their interest. Most of them spent the time looking at things quite outside their chosen subject of study. Then it was time to go home. Should the museum have chosen not to have a children's department, it is essential to go there first in order to plan the work. Her Majesty's Stationery Office issue a booklet, *Guide to London Museums and Galleries*, which is a great help in deciding where to go in London, or else there is a descriptive list at the back of the A–Z Street Guide. Teachers everywhere can profit by reading Barbara Winstanley's book, *Children and Museums* (Blackwell), which discusses at length the value of these visits for children and the kind of work they can do.

A common misconception about excursions to places of historical interest is that the objects seen will in themselves have some meaning for the children, whether they are visiting a museum, a piece of architecture, or a ruin. What could be better, if they have been studying the Roman army, than to show them the remains of a Roman fort, or a piece of Roman armour? In actual fact, to relate these things to life as it was once lived, which is surely the aim, requires an immense imaginative effort. A piece of Roman armour will remain a piece of metal, and a prehistoric flint, however rare, will remain a lump of old stone, unless children can make this imaginative leap. I always think this is particularly difficult in the case of ruined remains like a castle, or an abbey. What connection can the crumbling stones of an abbey, or the deserted, mossy remains of a Roman fort possibly have with the busy, bustling life that once went on there? Children need to do the necessary recreative thinking before they go on such a visit, if it is to mean anything to them. They should be given a great deal of historical background. If they are to see the remains of a Roman villa, they should have a picture in their minds of the Roman way of life in its full glory, so that the Roman baths, the crumbling mosaics, the vents for central heating, really are links with a vital past. Once on the site, they should have a clearly defined objective, relating to this vision.

If the school excursion centres on a building, such as one of the great surviving houses of the past, or a cathedral, then the visit is somewhat easier for the building itself is a focus and provides a firm contact for the life that was lived in it. In many of these monuments guided tours are provided, carefully adjusted to the party's age group. Some provide nobly for the needs of children. Just one example is *Let's Explore St Alban's Abbey*, by David Pepin, who has now written 20 similar guidebooks for different cathedrals and churches. These are available at church bookstalls, and a page from the St Alban's guide is reproduced opposite. There is a short, clear explanation of the legend of St Alban, descriptions of points of interest which can be seen during a walk round, pictures to colour, and even a crossword. St Alban's also has a tape for classroom use before school visits, and a cut-out model of the Abbey can be bought at the bookstall.

Sometimes, though, I feel that visitors do not get as rich an impression as they might from some of these excursions, because they look only for the obvious. A cathedral is a monument to Christianity, but also to much else. Inside many of our churches are to be seen, not only the splendid architecture and stained glass, but also, usually in the choir-stalls, the faces of our mediaeval ancestors and even a hob-goblin or two, carved hundreds of years ago by some craftsman who, through a devout church-goer, remained haunted by his older beliefs. These details give the monument its human setting. Children should be allowed to keep open minds and to look around them sensitively. If given a chance, they ask their own questions. They will want to know why the floors of old buildings are uneven, and how the colours were made for the stained glass. They can inspire some lively research.

I have left until last the discussion of music, as it is an original source in a category all by itself. Music stands apart from other creative endeavour, having its own unique medium, and musicians naturally grow angry when people of other disciplines suggest that it can be treated as an ancillary to other subjects. While nobody would suggest that we should sit and listen to the music of Handel solely with a view to what it might tell us about the eighteenth century, nevertheless the music of a given period is inextricably bound up

Stand beneath the **TOWER** and **LOOK** up. The Normans also built this. How solid-looking it is! The painted ceiling is nearly 103 feet above you. This TOWER has a peal of 12 bells.

LOOK at the fine ROUNDED NORMAN ARCHES.

LOOK at the CHOIR. Here the monks used to praise God day and night. The daily services are still held here.

LOOK at the BISHOP'S THRONE.

LOOK at the PRESBYTERY.

LOOK at the HOLY TABLE, called the HIGH ALTAR, with the beautiful stone REREDOS or SCREEN rising high above it.

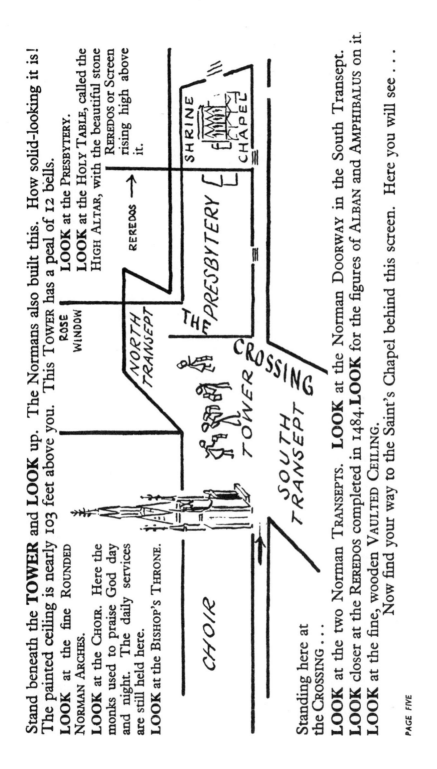

REREDOS →

ROSE WINDOW

NORTH TRANSEPT

THE PRESBYTERY

CROSSING

TOWER

SOUTH TRANSEPT

CHOIR

SHRINE

CHAPEL

Standing here at the CROSSING . . .

LOOK at the two Norman TRANSEPTS. **LOOK** at the Norman DOORWAY in the South Transept.

LOOK closer at the REREDOS completed in 1484. **LOOK** for the figures of ALBAN and AMPHIBALUS on it.

LOOK at the fine, wooden VAULTED CEILING.

Now find your way to the Saint's Chapel behind this screen. Here you will see . . .

A page from Let's Explore St Alban's Abbey, *by David Pepin* with all other aspects of human existence, and as such is a valuable historical source. It relates often to the dance and costume of a time, as does the minuet, or to its religious spirit, as witness the great Masses of the sixteenth century. It can even relate to the material resources of a period in history. After all, the complicated trills of much sixteenth century music were in part a necessity brought about by the lack of a musical instrument possessing a sustained note. Apart from all this, the music of an age conveys something more, for it conveys its atmosphere. Children, when they listen to it, are hearing the thoughts of a human being who lived in a time other than their own, albeit these thoughts are expressed in musical terms. This applies to so-called classical music; folk music has also the medium of words. The songs the people of the past sang about their lives tell us a great deal about them. These are discussed more fully in the next chapter, on audio-visual aids. Topic Records Ltd (see page 153) are performing a great service to schools, for they are reviving many of these folk-songs and are reproducing them in recorded form, specially for use in the teaching of history.

Another way of bringing pupils into touch with many kinds of original sources is through local history. This has become an increasingly popular study in recent years, not merely in schools but also among many adults as a hobby. It may be that, as local boundaries slip away, our local traditions become more precious to us, giving us a sense of identity. Or perhaps it is part of the same urge to return to essentials that is behind the movement to introduce original historical material in the classroom. Whatever the reason, more and more schools are taking up local studies.

Local history may be defined as the study of a particular geographical area and it can be approached in several different ways. Sometimes, local events can serve as a vivid illustration of events that took place on a national scale, as when an army on the march to some great battle camped in a particular spot, or when the local village was racked by enclosure. Or else local history can be studied for its own sake, and even here there are various ways of working. A theme can be taken, such as the growth of transport in the area, or the changing pattern of building, resulting in a 'line of development' study. Or an intensive study can be made of every aspect of life at a given point in time, resulting in a survey of the 'patch' kind.

Whichever way of working is adopted, local history holds a great deal for children, and a rightful place in the classroom. Its greatest appeal lies in its quality of immediacy. Its material is all around us, in the roads we tread, in the houses we live in and in the open spaces in which we play. Children often have a sneaking suspicion that history does not really exist, but a local study can convince them that it does. After all, they can often trace on an old map the very road along which they walked to school. This is particularly valuable with children of limited ability, who find it reassuring to work with material they can actually see.

Allied to this sense of conviction that it carries, local history can possess an almost aesthetic quality. It can redeem the ugliness of an area, and in doing so give comfort and dignity to the people who live in it. This is a great help when one is teaching children in a poverty-stricken area, for apart from encouraging them to hold their heads high, it makes them eager to work. I taught some years ago in a school which drew most of its children from a rough area in south-east London. It would be difficult to imagine an uglier or more congested street than its main shopping centre, crowded with traffic, cheap shops and fumes from the local factories. Yet this same street had been a thoroughfare for hundreds of years; the peasant farmers of long ago drove their cattle along it to Smithfield. The cheap little shops had been built in the spacious front gardens of the well-to-do houses of the eighteenth and nineteenth centuries. These facts were of great interest to the children, and they were also considerably amused by the discovery of the remains of a prehistoric fish beneath the public house where many of their fathers were wont to drink in the evenings. This kind of knowledge gives children background; it makes their tread firmer.

A local study has other virtues. It makes possible study in depth, both of people and places, which is often not possible as we skate through history on a national scale. There are opportunities for ways of working which seem more in keeping with children's natural ways of thinking than the more conventional methods. The barriers between subjects break down when one is working in one's immediate environment, for geological, historical and biological factors cannot be separated from one another. The barrier between school and home is likewise broken down, for the children are continually drawing upon their home environment to provide working material in school. Often children come to have a feeling for their own community that they did not possess before, and a willingness to participate more in it. Somewhat unexpectedly, a study of local affairs has often a truer and more subtle bearing on present-day issues than does a study of national history. In studying the immediate neighbourhood, one comes to realise the nature of a community: how it has evolved, and how it can be changed. This is the essence of social criticism.

Local history can also give rise to a variety of work for children; apart from the implication that they shall get out and walk with purpose about their district, there is the opportunity to write, to draw and model and set out their findings in unusual ways. Lastly, children can find, in local history, the opportunity to study original sources, to see how history is made, and perhaps to make it themselves.

Nevertheless, there are some well-known pit-falls in this kind of work. If local history were studied in schools and nothing else, our children might be gold-mines of interesting facts such as that asparagus was grown in their district in the eighteenth century, and yet know nothing about the agricultural revolution. Local history can easily deteriorate into a study of minutiae. Another consideration is that it is easier to carry out a local study in some districts than in others; it is fascinating and rewarding in the City of London or in an ancient country village, but almost impossible on a council estate in a new town. Worst of all, there are few textbooks. The sources for local history are many and lie in varied places; they have to be hunted out and may not even be accessible at all; even if they are obtained, they may be difficult to understand. This means that the opportunity for children to work with original sources may be severely restricted. It also means a great deal of work for the teacher, who has to be the fount of knowledge for the class.

In spite of the drawbacks, many teachers find a local study well worthwhile. Before, however, one begins, one has to decide exactly what meaning the word 'local' shall have. Does it refer to the city in which one lives, one's own borough, or even one's street? Would a local study imply, for a Londoner, an investigation covering the whole of London? I think that the word 'local' refers to anything that is relevant in one's immediate environment; relevant, that is, to oneself. This will clearly be different for different people. One can safely generalise and say that its meaning will usually be much narrower for children, with their smaller horizons, than it will for grown-ups. For a child, his locality may mean just a few streets and the park where he plays, or even just his own home. The younger he is, the narrower his horizon will be. This is an important point, for it means one must take care to match the extent of one's project to the age and interests of one's class.

One also has to decide on the meaning of the world 'local' in another sense. Does it imply a study of the physical environment, or something more? It seems to me that what is implied in local history is the study of a community. This applies whatever kind of method one is using; if one is illuminating a particular episode in national history by using local resources, one is really looking at a smaller community at a particular moment; if one is taking one line of development, like transport, one is studying the effect that development had on the life of the whole; if the survey method is used, all the factors that play a part in the evolution of a community are taken and analysed. This way of looking at the subject has most meaning for the child; history is, after all, about people.

Having decided all this, the teacher is ready to begin. Several valuable books are available. There is *Local History and the Teacher* by R. Douch (Routledge and Kegan Paul), and T. H. Corfe's book *History in the Field*, a field study handbook for teachers, from Holt-Blond (Blond) Educational). Both these books list the sources of local history and give examples of how they can be used in the classroom. *How to Find Out in History* by P. Hepworth (Pergamon) is a survey of all the sources available to the historian, with a particularly good section on local history. There is at present a wave of interest in local history, and publishers and other organisations are responding to the need. Ginn publish a series of books under the title *Discovering your Environment*, several of which, such as *History in a Village, History in Towns,* and *History along Roads and Waterways,* provide useful clues and background for local study.

The Education Unit of the Town and Country Planning Association publishes *BEE* (Bulletin of Environmental Education), a monthly bulletin for teachers. Its emphasis is on the urban environment, though other aspects of environmental teaching are also covered. It gives guidance on available sources and resources, suggests teaching ideas and methods, and offers material for class use. It can be a great help in the survey-type of local study.

Any teacher intending to embark on a study of local history must read up the subject first. The number of primary sources, if one chooses to begin with them, is often very great, consisting of maps, buildings, archives, pictorial records and newspapers, among others. They may often be difficult to track down, although some counties, such as Essex and Oxfordshire, print comprehensive lists of all the sources available for their locality. Because there is this difficulty, it is often better to begin by reading a general history of the area one intends to cover. This often provides a great deal of information and useful starting-points. The Victoria County History is the best background reading for the counties; often, too, the local history society, whether in town or country district, is a mine of information and will provide a short outline history of its own locality. Sometimes one is lucky and finds that an enthusiast has written a really good local history that is simple and clear enough for the children to use by themselves. This is so in my own area, where a fascinating book has just been written by a local teacher. Sadly, books of this kind are few and far between, for the simple reason that, having an appeal to only a limited number of readers, they are not a commercially viable proposition. Be that as it may, making contact with the local society, and a visit to the public library, are both essential.

The teacher in a city can usually uncover a lot of information. This is certainly the case with London. There is the comprehensive *Discovering London* (Macdonald & Co), which covers in eight volumes, reasonably priced, the history of London from Roman to modern times. The same publisher produces a series of mini-guides to London, with volumes on Roman, Medieval and Tudor London, among others. Armed with these, one could begin the study with a guided tour. Then there is Rasmussen's *London the Unique City*, published by Penguin, which tells the story of London through the ages. There is even an excellent textbook written for children, *History of London*, by J. Hayes (Black), attractively written and illustrated.

As one reads about the background of the locality that is to be studied, certain ways in which the children can work suggest themselves. These are different in the case of each locality, each teacher and each group of children, so that what follows is in the nature of the broadest of suggestions. There are certain approaches to local history that normally prove popular with children, though these have to be adapted to various levels of ability and to the varying lengths of time available for the study.

Most children are very conscious of territory. Like cats, their busy lives are lived within well-marked boundaries, which they take care to pace and re-pace regularly, almost ritually, though with a deceptively casual air. This being so, the territorial approach to a local study is a good one. It appeals to most children to begin their work with a survey of the physical features of their environment as it is at present. One can begin by taking them for a walk, noticing outstanding features. How are the houses positioned, for example? Is there a river nearby, or a railway, or any marked physical features, such as hills and valleys? These observations are just as revealing in towns as they are of country districts. I know a densely populated area in inner London which is all hills, valleys and little streams under the concrete. That is how it actually was, two hundred years ago. Other points to notice are the kinds of trees and plants that grow naturally, the soil formation and the climate. Having noted the salient physical features of their environment, the children can begin, with guidance, to see their explanation. In such a study, maps are essential. The Ordnance Survey maps are most useful, the one-inch to one-mile maps particulary so, as they give information as to both phsycial and human geography. The larger maps, 25 inches to 1 mile, are valuable in a detailed investigation, as they show individual streets, houses and boundaries, as well as giving historical information. The Ordnance Survey has made an interesting attempt to reconstruct past landscapes; already published are the maps of Ancient Britain, Southern Britain in the Iron Age, Roman Britain, Britain in the Dark Ages, and Monastic Britain. The Ordnance Survey (see page 153) will send on request a list of its agents throughout the country, from which maps may be purchased. Another source of maps for its district is the local public library, which may well possess old maps, also original prints and pictures which illuminate certain features. Libraries and museums are sometimes willing to lend these precious possessions to schools, or to accept small parties of children to study them, provided, of course, that they are scrupulously cared for while on loan. A useful way with the Ordnance Survey maps, or any that would not be harmed by being handled in this way, is to trace them on transparent paper and then stick them together in book form, with the oldest at the bottom and the most recent on top. If the maps are traced boldly in different colours—for example, red for the Stone Age, blue for the Middle Ages and so on—as the pages are turned they present almost a moving picture of how the locality has evolved. I saw this done recently with maps of a district and one fact emerged most vividly, that the highways and byways along which people had travelled had for centuries remained the same, always traversing the same hills and avoiding certain difficult terrain, until the arrival of the motorway, which cut directly across these ancient ways and, it was clear, the habits of the community. A striking change in the life of the community was thus shown visually.

Another approach that children generally enjoy in local history is through names. Local names nearly always incorporate the history of a district; this applies to the names of people, buildings and streets. It is rare now to find a village where the inhabitants share between them just a few surnames, though

78

this still applies to outlying districts like the Scilly Isles. More frequently the names of people who played an outstanding part in the history of a locality are commemorated in streets, and sometimes parks. In the post-industrial era, many new urban streets took the names of the great families upon whose estates they were built. Sometimes, one can even find living testimony of this in the trees that still survive in tiny back gardens. For instance, I know of a stretch of dreary back streets in a city area where nearly every tiny garden has a lilac tree, surviving, I suspect, from the estate from whose grounds they were parcelled out. Place names provide many historical clues. They can illustrate the origins of early settlers, the ways in which the inhabitants were wont to earn their living, or features of the landscape, as well as commemorating famous people. Street names can denote trade or occupation, as in the famous Pudding Lane, or perhaps a well-known building, as in 'Church Street', or the character of a street, as in 'Sandy Lane' and 'Broad Street'. Children enjoy collecting names and investigating them.

From research into street names, the study of buildings arises naturally. The important and famous buildings usually speak for themselves, but it is a pity to restrict the study to these. The humble houses, where the ordinary people lived out their lives, tell just as much history. Why were they built where they were? Were they built of local materials? What kind of life was lived in them?

Perhaps the most fascinating source of all for local history is through people. This includes not merely the great names associated with a district, but people who are alive today. Change takes place so rapidly nowadays that most of us have valuable memories. Local tradesmen, doctors, park-keepers and librarians, and also the local policeman, can often produce valuable information, and many of these are surprisingly willing to come and talk in a friendly way with children. This is a good way of approaching the subject with very young children, for nothing is so convincing as the person who can actually remember himself. Sometimes one comes across an unexpected goldmine. Recently a very old man came up to mend my fence. There is near us a broad main road, with the houses on one side having very much larger front gardens than those on the other. During the course of conversation the old man explained that this was because a trout stream had once flowed through what was now the long front gardens, in which he had fished as a boy. The ground was too soft to build. on. In his youth, the busy main road was a place of fields and streams. He further told us that when our own houses had been built, on previously uninhabited woodland, the excavators found some strange tunnels, but nobody knew what they were. Here then was a vivid picture painted of the past, and a question to be answered.

Persuading people to talk in this way to very young children, and allowing the children themselves to collect information from people they know, is a vivid way of introducing them to local history. Even if they collect a few tall stories, as they undoubtedly will, it will be an interesting way of teaching them to sift the wheat from the chaff, an essential ability in the historian.

Places, names and people, then, are colourful sources of local history. I would like, however, to end this discussion with a plea for a new approach to this kind of work in our towns and cities. Often, a local study in the busy borough of a town turns into a kind of exercise in nostalgia, the 'Oh for the day when our streets were green fields' kind of approach. A very important aspect of local history is often virtually ignored, and that is its industry. This is all the more serious when you consider that at least four-fifths of us live in towns and that we are an industrial nation. A rich source of history lies here waiting to be explored. Many big firms possess a great deal of interesting original material about their own industries, some have written their own histories and many are very generous to school-children. I once saw a local history project carried out with a group of children, based on the history of a local factory in which many of their fathers worked. The history of the factory mirrored, not only social developments in the immediate area, but the coming of the Industrial Revolution itself. The children were received very kindly at the factory by the personnel officer and workers alike, and one cannot help feeling that many other business enterprises would be equally pleased to meet the schools in this way. This kind of approach has the virtue of having a vital bearing on life today.

There now remains the problem of what materials the children can use in the classroom when working on a local history project. First of all, there are two books which children themselves can use in planning their work. They have been written specially to help children in work of this kind. *Topic Know-How* by W. H. Shaw (Blackwell) tells the reader what kind of information he will need, the questions he should ask in order to receive answers of value, and how to set out his findings. *Introducing Local Studies* by J. K. Dale (Dent) has been written expressly for children between the ages of nine and thirteen. The B.B.C. has also entered the field of local history with its broadcasts of the history of an imaginary town, raising the kind of issue that emerges in most local studies.

Much of the work the children will do will take place outside school, but still they need a supply of good reference books with which to supplement their findings in the classroom. An excellent series of little books, *History from Familiar Things* by Stephen Usherwood (Ginn), has been produced in order to do precisely this. There are books on place names, street names, festivals and holidays, coins, and inns and inn signs; each is accompanied by a project book. There is also a need for children to have access to reference books concerning anything they might observe during the course of their work, such as people's occupations, modes of transport, and homes. Shire Publications publish an interesting series of *Discovering Books*, which are a great help to children in local studies. These cheaply priced little books include *Discovering Inn Signs*, *Discovering Wall Paintings*, *This Old House*, *Discovering Castles* and many more. The titles of these books explain their object, which is to help children explore the world about them. If children also read a general social history, this will illuminate many of the apparently disconnected facts they might collect, and weave them into a coherent picture.

One always hopes, when working on local history, that the class will have the opportunity of working from original archive material. You may be lucky, for some local authorities, such as Essex and Buckinghamshire, and some universities, such as Newcastle, produce folders of original material including documents, maps, pictures and photographs compiled specially for children. The University of Sheffield Institute of Education is also publishing local history pamphlets which aim at providing a microcosm of national developments through a particular topic of local interest. For example, the titles so far produced include *Bronze Age Man in Derbyshire* by J. P. Heathcote, which illustrates the technical achievements of the Bronze Age through findings in Derbyshire.

Often the local library or museum is willing to lend children, or at least let them see, collections of documents, old prints and photographs. Cities such as Bristol, Leicester and York have special folk museums which use material remains from which to reconstruct scenes of local life from other times. As has already been said, maps can be obtained from the Ordnance Survey.

But it may be that such valuable help is not at hand. Then the teacher has the choice of confining the study to secondary sources, or of hunting down the original sources himself. Briefly, you may expect to find local archives in the following places, though a comprehensive list is given in the book by Robert Douch (*Local History and the Teacher*, published by Routledge and Kegan Paul). The parish records, often to be found in the County Records Offices, concern such subjects as poor relief from the seventeenth to the early nineteenth century, the accounts of officials (for example, the church-warden, the constable, and the surveyor of highways), and records of baptisms, marriages and deaths. The County Records Office houses material concerning the Courts of Quarter Sessions, fairs, parliamentary elections and enclosures. This is where one would begin if one were studying crime in the district, the effect of the enclosure movement, and so on. Large boroughs look after their own archives, and in the record office of a large borough is to be found all the material concerning municipal administration, such as borough income, privileges, trade and the guilds. Bishops' registers and documents concerning the behaviour of laity and clergy are to be found either in the Diocesan Record Office, or among the county records. Apart from all these sources, there are many private collections. Her Majesty's Stationery Office publishes annually a *List of Accessions to Repositories*, which lists the owners of records, their content and under what conditions they are available. It is wise to look through this for anything that concerns one's own district.

These archives are the material from which the professional historian works. Are there ways in which they can be brought into the classroom for children to work on themselves? One must say at once that many of these documents are too difficult for children to use unaided for, apart from the strange handwriting, before the sixteenth century they are likely to be written in Latin. It may be necessary for the teacher to paraphrase those that can be used for the class to understand them. This could at least be done for one or two important documents, and the result cyclo-styled for general use. Such work, though, means a considerable burden for the individual teacher. The longterm solution for the provision of original documents for use in schools lies probably in photo-statting. Some offices already do this, though it is apt to prove expensive.

There is another very cheering possibility, and that is that the teachers of groups of local schools, interested in introducing their children to this work, shall get together and form a kind of cooperative enterprise. If the searching out and reproducing of material were shared in this way, the work would be greatly reduced and I am sure would prove great fun. In fact there is a great need for this kind of venture for much broader reasons, for one of the things wrong with the schools at the moment is not only their isolation from the community outside, but also their isolation from each other. Quite often the teachers of one school are quite unaware of what is going on in another school quite near.

A great new movement is taking place in local history. There is an enormous revival of interest, not only among ,individuals but among local authorities, universities and archivists as well. Much original material is being collected and made available to the public for the first time, and it is becoming clear that much of our local history is still waiting to be discovered and written up. It would be a great thing if our schoolchildren could take part in this adventure.

5
Audio-Visual Aids and the Teaching of History

The senses are the interpreters of the mind, bringing it information from the outside world. It is on this relationship, between the mind and the senses, that the value of audio-visual aids in teaching is based. It is not a simple relationship, though it might seem so at first. For one thing, a purely objective impression from the outside world does not exist. When the senses relay information to the mind, the mind acts upon it, forming it into a complex made up of material gleaned in other ways, and of the total needs of the individual. But the next time the senses relay that same piece of information, the mind will react differently, for it will now take into account its past experience and, very probably, different needs. In this way, perception is modified. We see, not with our eyes, but with our minds as well. The longer we live, the more this is so, for we have a much fuller experience to draw upon. By the time a child comes to see a visual aid in the class-room, his reaction will be intensely individual. This is a very important point, for it means that each child's reactions are likely to be different, and that teaching aids must be used in such a way as to allow scope for individuality.

Another point must be made here. In discussing the role of audio-visual aids in teaching, we are concerned with their role in promoting thinking. We do not mean to provide in our lessons a continual stream of sensuous experiences, and leave it at that. We mean to use these impressions as an aid to learning our subject. They are, in fact, what they claim to be—'aids'. It is fascinating to reflect that not all the senses bear the same relationship to the mind in this role of promoting thought. By far the most sensitive and vivid are the senses of sight and hearing. No one, so far as I know, has attempted to devise comprehensive teaching aids based on the senses of smell and touch. The reason seems to be that the impressions of smell and touch are incapable of abstraction, whereas those of sight and sound are capable of being turned into the tools of thought. In this lies their intrinsic value to teaching.

What concerns us here especially is how this relationship between the senses and the mind can be exploited in the teaching of our own subject, history. In what ways can audio-visual aids enable us to teach history better? Can they help a child in the formation of historical judgement? I think that it is generally agreed that in many ways they can.

Visual aids are far more commonly used in the classroom than audio aids, probably because what we see makes the most vivid impression of all. We will therefore discuss them first, although much of what follows applies to both.

Visual aids, by which is meant pictures, slides, films and television, have, in the first place, an enormous contribution to make in the realm of accurate, factual knowledge. They can bring to children objects of rare historical value that they might otherwise never see. We may not be able to provide fossils for them to handle, certainly most of us have never seen a Ming vase or handled the precious jewellery of ancient Sumer, but the picture or film can bring these things into the classroom. It is not quite the same as actually having these things, but it is the next best thing. The film or overhead projector is particularly useful in illustrating a process. A film showing the working of Jethro Tull's seed-drill or James Watt's steam engine explains them more clearly than anything we can say, and with the kind of accurate detail that cannot be put into words. In this sense, visual aids in the history lesson come as near as possible to providing actual experience of the past.

Frequently, the picture or film can actually prevent misunderstanding. One often hears the view that history is a literary subject and can only be expressed in verbal concepts, but hardly ever is it pointed out that these very words are open to misunderstanding. In history, many words have different meanings according to the periods of time to which they refer. 'Transport' means something different in almost every century, from the beginning of time onwards. So does 'shop', 'village' and 'town'. The differences are much more clearly shown by illustration than by any amount of verbal exposition. On these occasions, the visual aid is a more accurate source of information than the book.

Because of this, the visual aid has a vital contribution to make in helping the child to think historically. The first essential to any kind of thinking is accurate knowledge, and pictures and films can provide this abundantly. Without this accuracy, the imaginative reconstruction of the past and the formation of complexes of historical facts, which in turn lead to a sense of historical development, are a difficult matter, if not impossible. Visual aids have a further advantage in that they bring an element of the concrete into learning, giving the mind raw material with which to work. It is well known that the first stage in the development of thinking is the handling of the concrete, and that abstract thinking follows. In giving a child a picture or an object in the history lesson, one is allowing him to think simply, with easily-handled tools. This is particularly valuable with children who for some reason cannot handle words easily, whether because they are backward, or not conversant with the language because they are immigrant or just lacking in verbal ability; perhaps they are merely very young. Sometimes teachers are worried by the thought that if they provide too much visual material for a child to work with, he will then not bother to work in any other way, remaining fettered to the concrete, perhaps for ever. I doubt very much whether this ever actually happens. As soon as a child has finished with pictures and their like, as soon as he can carry impressions in his mind and dispense with the need to have objects physically before him in order to think, he will do so. He will enter, when he is ready, the more abstract, and in many ways more subtle, world of books. Pictures and films do not retard the use of the written or spoken word. Often the opposite is true, and they will stimulate a child to burst into writing, or at least into speech.

Because the human mind is so sensitive to visual impression, visual aids have a specialised part to play in the teaching of history. An essential part of learning history is the ability to remember. Unless we have this ability, we cannot form the associations of historical facts which are necessary for the development of time-sense and perspective. In the old days learning dates off by heart was a favourite exercise in the history lesson. Nowadays, we have a deeper understanding of the faculty of memory. We realise that remembering is a complex matter, based on understanding. However, there are still times when it is essential to be able to carry facts in the mind, even on quite a superficial level, for, at the very least, in history they form a framework into which one can fit more important things. This is where visual aids can often help. It is well known that some people have exceptional visual memories— they are those who can glance at a page of a book and then repeat it, word for word. The rest of us remember facts visually to a certain extent. For this reason, it is often helpful to set historical facts out in a visual form, to make a pattern for the mind, so to speak. Most teachers do this subconsciously when they write up headings on the blackboard, or produce a chart depicting some great historical movement. They are giving the facts a visual pattern, so that they may be remembered.

One can exploit the visual element in memorising in other ways. I once had a class of backward eleven-year-olds, who were making a study of pre-history. I wanted them to be able to remember, not only when the various forms of life came on earth, but also what accompanied them; for example that in the Carboniferous Age there were great trees in the swamps, the first amphibians and insects, and that the climate was warm and moist. I therefore made them a hardboard chart which I could use at the front of the class, and into which I could slide pieces of card giving the relevant facts. I kept a different colour for everything associated with a particular time—red for Cambrian, black for Carboniferous (when coal was formed) and so on. Colour plays an important part in visual memory. When actually asking the children to memorise the facts, I would leave the cards in for perhaps a minute, before removing them. The shorter and sharper the visual impact is, the longer it stays in the mind. Sometimes I jumbled up the cards and asked one of the children to slide them into the appropriate slots. They enjoyed this game and one can think of many variations of it. These visual images remain in the mind for many years; I can still see that chart myself, to this day.

Period	Animals and plants	Climate	
Cambrian	Sea plants and sea creatures without backbones	Cold	(Red background)
Carboniferous	Amphibians, insects (including dragon-flies), ferns	Warm	(Black background)
Jurassic	Dinosaurs and other reptiles, conifers	Warm and damp	(Yellow background)

Pictures, film-strips and film can help children to develop the intellectual components of a historical sense. They are sources of accurate knowledge, they help the child to associate historical facts relevantly, they help him to remember. They make things easier for the child who cannot handle words. They possess one other great asset, in that they can bring to the history lesson a rare imaginative quality. Imagine a picture, for example, of the mediaeval peasantry. The people in their rough clothes, with their toughened drawn faces and gnarled hands, can express most poignantly something of what it must have been like to live and work in a subsistence economy. In this way, a picture can add to the intellectual content of history teaching, for it can express the very atmosphere of an age. Films can convey this emotional quality to an even greater extent, for here sound, vision and spoken commentary can reinforce each other. It is important to realise that this emotional impact is closely connected with intellectual effort. The impression made on a child by a really good film or picture can give him the stimulus to find out more in a strictly intellectual sense, to progress, say, from sympathy with those hard-pressed people, to a knowledge of the elusive factors that lay behind their lives.

Having discussed the admittedly very great contributions visual aids can make to the teaching of history, we ought now to consider the other side of the coin. Are they in any sense limited? Can they help a child's developing sense of history in the fullest possible way? Are they in any sense dangerous?

I think, firstly, that it is true to say that a visual aid cannot replace, or develop, certain thought processes. A picture or a film can make a vivid concrete impression, it can help a child to build up a factual association, it can convey atmosphere, and all this is essential to the learning of history, but there it stops. It can only convey very clumsily the relationship between cause and effect; it cannot, by itself, give a sense of development, of evolution in time; it cannot help the child evaluate people and events, for values can only be expressed in words; its constitution, by its very nature, is usually limited to the concrete. It has been said by an eminent critic of television, Milton Shulman, that 'it tells how, but not why', and this, I think, is a fair general comment on the value of visual aids.

The impossibility of portraying cause and effect visually can be seen by considering television and films. Suppose we have a producer who intends to show the causes of the American colour problem. To portray this in words would be difficult enough, but to portray it in terms of vision infinitely more so. For one thing, the producer has an infinitely greater choice of pictures than he does of words. This makes his final selection at once cruder and more liable to distortion. He might well begin his programme with a flash of negroes voting in New York, then show the poverty in which they live and then perhaps show a white American giving his views about 'the blacks'. But this would be a crude analysis and would need to be accompanied by a careful verbal account, for certain things can only be expressed in words. Logical, conceptual thinking is one. Time-sense is another. A few bars of music, a clock ticking away—skilful cutting in a film can be used effectively to express the actual passage of time, but historical time-sense in terms of development can only be expressed verbally. Words also have advantages totally lacking in mere visual impact. They can express the abstract—concepts like 'thought', 'meaning' and 'dishonesty'—whereas vision can only express the concrete. A visual impression invariably involves generalisation, whereas words can express the delicate and particular. Words, furthermore, embody past experience and a wealth of imagery lacking to vision. This gives them a subtle perspective. Speech is, therefore, in many cases a much speedier mode of communication than vision. Take a sentence I have before me, 'Mr. Brown called the meeting.' How speedily it is put into words, and what a cumbersome series of shots on film it would take to achieve the same effect. It must be accepted then that visual aids by themselves cannot be used to develop certain thought processes vital to the historian, those of time-sense and development, of forming judgements, of dealing with the abstract. 'Thought,' it has been said, 'is internalised speech.'

Further, there is a danger inherent in the very vividness of the impression that a film or picture can make. It can show the 'how' so vividly that one is no longer concerned with the 'why'. Most of us will probably have experienced this feeling while watching television. We sit there entranced with the wealth of visual images flashed before our eyes and we stop thinking. If the visual impression is wrong, as well as vivid, the harm done is even greater. This was the case, a year or two back, with a schools television programme about the Duke of Wellington, who won the Battle of Waterloo. There are portraits of the Duke, so that we know what he looked like, but an actor quite different in physique appeared on the screen. The children who watched that programme may well now carry in their minds a completely wrong idea of what the Duke looked like. This is, in my opinion, an example of the wrong use of a visual aid.

Perhaps, then, one should bear in mind certain considerations when using visual aids. They should be used sparingly, exactly for the purpose for which one requires them. This should be thought out carefully beforehand. The use of illustrative material should be carefully integrated with the rest of one's work, so that the film or broadcast should not appear to be the reason for the lesson, but the other way round. Children should not be allowed to wallow in visual aids, nor to become drugged by them, but should be continually encouraged to write and to talk. Individual differences between children should also always be borne in mind. Everybody's reactions to a visual aid is likely to be different, for the reasons discussed at the beginning of the chapter, and it should also be remembered that not everybody thinks visually to the same extent. Visual aids should therefore always be used in such a way as to allow full scope for individual differences.

One last temptation lurks behind the wealth of pictures, films, slides and film strips that exist today. It is the temptation for the teacher to retire behind them and to abdicate from the responsibility of teaching. But visual aids make the responsibility of the teacher greater, not less, for he or she has the added task of weaving them, together with all the other resources that exist in teaching today, into a meaningful whole. They are, as they claim to be, 'aids'.

The teacher today can draw on many audio-visual resources. They all depend on the relationship between the senses of sight and sound and the mind in the first place, and then on the relationship between the impressions the mind has received and verbal thinking. People have thought up ways of exploiting these relationships, without expressing the assumptions that they are making scientifically. Sometimes a visual impression is accompanied by a spoken explanation, as with films and filmstrips. Sometimes a visual impression is given just by itself, as when we simply show a picture. Recently there has been a trend towards combining the film-strip with the written word, as in the *Then and There* series (Longman). The B.B.C. has thought of yet another variation, for it is producing film-strips to be used in conjunction with its sound broadcasts. This 'radio-vision' service was begun experimentally in 1963–4; it has since been considerably extended and there are available numbers of radio-vision programmes on historical themes. New series are being added annually; there is also the possibility that radio-vision material may be available to accompany a radio programme (for example, 'History in Focus'—page 96). Information is available from the School Broadcasting Council for the United Kingdom (see page 154).

Some of the assumptions behind audio-visual aids need to be investigated. If we show a picture to a group of children, what effect does it have, if any, on their kind of thinking? Does it make any difference if we show a picture before letting children read about a subject, or after it? Can the differences between the audio and the visual aid, and there are many, be investigated? And what about that magical quality, imagination—how does the audio-visual aid relate to this? Possibly there is no answer to this kind of question, because human reactions are almost impossible to quantify and individual reactions, being unique, mean that generalisations are often impossible to make. However, these questions need to be continually asked.

I should like now to proceed to a brief discussion of the various individual aids available to the history teacher. Strangely enough, the most important is the one that is most frequently forgotten. It is the blackboard. It stands in every class-room, however poorly equipped this may be in other ways, yet its use is hardly ever thought about, and very rarely practised. It has a variety of uses. If one has a gift for rapid drawing, it can provide a vivid and often amusing accompaniment to a verbal exposition. It can be used as an aid to memory, in much the same way as the hardboard chart was used with children studying prehistory. It can be used to give words a visual pattern so that they can be more easily understood.

The most important use of the blackboard is to use it as a way of analysing a mass of material and reducing it to order. One does this when one writes the most important points of a subject up on the board. In spite of all this, the blackboard is often used badly, and many of its possibilities remain unexplored. Many of us, it seems, are unaware that a messy blackboard imparts the same messiness and air of confusion to the thoughts of the children who are watching it. Some of us forget also that what is written on the board should be seen without strain from any other point in the room. Surprisingly, very little experiment has been carried out regarding the use of colour on the blackboard. Coloured chalks are available, though not used as often as they might be; another possibility is the use of variously coloured boards. We accept that we write with white chalk on a black board too easily, for other variations would be exciting and even easier to see. It has been shown, for instance, that the eye registers blue on a yellow background more easily than white on black. And what about using different coloured boards for different topics? An interesting field waits here for the enterprising teacher.

Another fruitful source of visual aids for the history lesson lies in the work of the teacher's own hands. Models can be made for demonstration purposes; it is surprising the effect they have on children and they need not be complicated. A ship can be made of cardboard, or a figure from wire netting, dressed to illustrate a costume. Alternatively, models can be bought. For example, there are excellent working models of the steam engine available.

There are so many sources of pictures, films, film-strips and recordings these days that several books have been published with information as to how to obtain them. The *Treasure Chest for Teachers*, published by the Schoolmaster Publishing Company, really is, as it says, a treasure chest, and is remarkably cheap. It gives the addresses of companies, embassies and societies which provide illustrative material suitable for schools on all kinds of subjects, and also speakers. Some publications give information regarding audio-visual aids for special fields of history. Several of these deserve mention, as they cover aspects of history frequently studied in schools for which audio-visual aids are often hard to find. The American Arts Documentation Centre, University of Exeter, issues *Audio-Visual Material for American Studies* (revised edition compiled by M. Gidley). Educational Audio-Visual Ltd (see page 152) produces a series of film-strips on modern European history, and as these are accompanied by recorded talks, they make an interesting combination. A Centaur Book, *Audio-Visual Aids Catalogue* by P. M. Jennings, sets out all the sources of teaching aids that are useful for any period in history. Lastly, the National Audio-Visual Aids Centre (see page 152) has a vast amount of material available from its library. This is outlined in a pamphlet which is sent to anybody on request.

After the blackboard, the most frequently used visual aid in the history lesson is the picture. Its great practical advantage is that it is easy to handle and store. Many pictures can be obtained free. Children's comics are a rich source, especially the boys' comics, which often produce series in colour on topics such as transport, or fighting men. For example, in one of its 1971 issues *The Hotspur* had a page entitled 'Funny Looks at Old 'Planes'. The drawings were accurate, amusing, and told a good story. Such pictures appeal to children, and many a happy hour can be spent cutting them out. Educational publications, such as the monthly *Pictorial Education*, nearly always include history pictures. Some firms and embassies are very generous in providing schools with material, the Russian and American embassies particularly so. Sometimes one of the larger banks will issue a chart, and the Post Office has available charts and pictures about the postal service.

Pictures specially for the history lesson were formerly produced by Macmillan Education who published four sets of full colour *History Class Pictures*, ranging from ancient to modern times, each picture large enough to fix on the blackboard for all to see. The sets are still (at the time of writing) reproduced in the form of booklets, called *History Picture Books*, which each child can use individually; each picture has a short explanation printed below it. These booklets make very good little textbooks for young or backward children.

Allied to the picture in some ways, but quite different in others, is the chart. The chart has all the practical advantages of the picture, but it depends on a verbal, as well as a visual, impression. Most historical charts, on close examination, emerge as analyses of their subjects. They set out topics that can really only be thought about in verbal terms. In so doing, they make them easier to grasp. An example, 'The Tudors', published by Pictorial Charts Educational Trust (see page 154) is reproduced on pages 92–3. The central achievement of the Tudors is placed firmly in the centre of the Tudor rose symbol; the most important actions of the Tudors are shown pictorially on the petals; portraits of the Tudor kings and queens are placed down one side of the chart. The whole is a skilful combination of words and visual appeal.

Film-strips can be used by themselves in the history lesson, or with a commentary spoken by the teacher, or they can be used in conjunction with a book. Blandford Press produces a series of books on world history, *World*

History in Colour by G. K. Tull and N. Heard, aimed at the adolescent; it is accompanied by film-strips. Showing a film-strip is a more adaptable process than showing a film because the pace of the lesson remains in the teacher's hands. He or she can adapt both the speed at which the pictures are shown and the pace of the commentary to the needs of the children in the class. There is a great deal to be said for encouraging the active and creative use of the film-strip by the children. It can be used as the basis for a 'patch' or a 'line of development' study, or it can be shown to the class and the children themselves asked to provide the commentary. It can, like many visual aids, be used as a stimulus to an interesting piece of research. Several firms produce very good film-strips for use in schools. There are the Rank Film Library and Educational Productions Ltd (for both, see page 152). Some film-strips cover a 'line of development' (for example, Rank's 'The Story of a Ship'), while others cover 'patch' subjects (for example, the reigns of great British monarchs). Nicholas Hunter Filmstrips (see page 152) have an excellent series on British social and economic history.

In contrast to a film-strip, a film has to be accepted in its entirety. It has to be seen straight through, and the pace is out of the teacher's control. The whole concept of the subject is also that of the producer. To this extent, the film is a less adaptable teaching aid than others. But herein also lies its strength, for the film is a complex form, combining several media: vision, music, and spoken commentary. The really good producer can combine these into a telling unity. He can make his film impart not merely knowledge but also mood and atmosphere and an implied comment on his subject. Apart from this special quality, the good film can bring into the class-room evidence that would not otherwise be seen and, because it is a moving picture, it can explain many processes more accurately than can be done in verbal exposition.

Many local education authorities have their own lending service of films for schools, free of charge. They vary in quality from the excellent to the mediocre. The trouble with films produced specially for children, as with any programmes come to that, is that they tend to lack bite. To an audience used to watching adult television programmes in the evening, some of the great events of history, thus produced, can seem rather tame.

Several big commercial firms lend films to schools free of charge. Among them are Shell, Unilever, and the Petroleum Films Bureau (for addresses, see page 152). As one would expect from the great oil companies, these films cover mainly prehistory. Some of the nationalised industries lend films and other visual aids on their own particular concerns; for example, the National Coal Board lends material on coal-mining (see page 152).

Much of what has been said about the film as an aid to history teaching applies also to the television broadcast. There are several important differences though, and one is that the television companies play their programmes yearly and so cannot be absolutely up to the minute. They also produce

'The Tudors', issued by Pictorial Charts Educational Trust

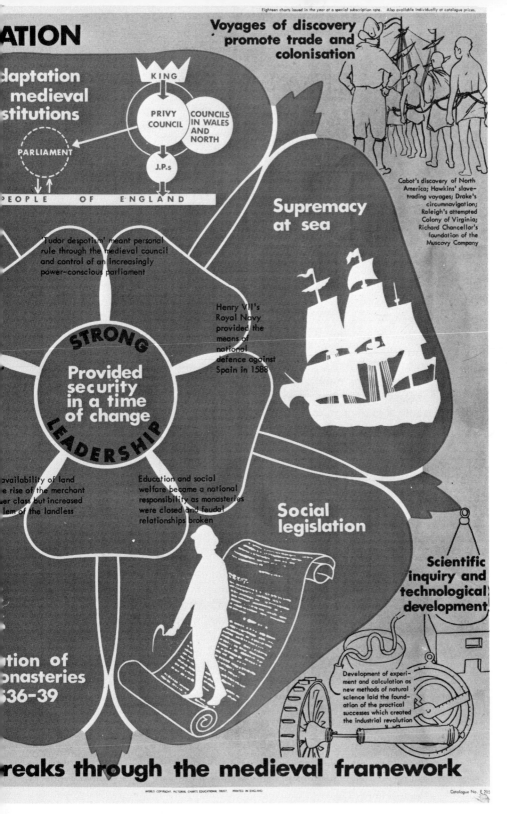

...ATION

...daptation
...medieval
...stitutions

**Voyages of discovery
promote trade and
colonisation**

KING

PRIVY
COUNCIL

COUNCILS
IN WALES
AND
NORTH

PARLIAMENT

J.P.s

...PEOPLE   OF   ENGLAND

Cabot's discovery of North
America; Hawkins' slave-
trading voyages; Drake's
circumnavigation;
Raleigh's attempted
Colony of Virginia;
Richard Chancellor's
foundation of the
Muscovy Company

'Tudor despotism' meant personal
rule through the medieval council
and control of an increasingly
power-conscious parliament

**Supremacy
at sea**

Henry VII's
Royal Navy
provided the
means of
national
defence against
Spain in 1588

STRONG
**Provided
security
in a time
of change**
LEADERSHIP

...availability of land
...e rise of the merchant
...er class but increased
...lem of the landless

Education and social
welfare became a national
responsibility as monasteries
were closed and feudal
relationships broken

**Social
legislation**

**Scientific
inquiry and
technological
development**

...tion of
...onasteries
...36-39

Development of experi-
ment and calculation as
new methods of natural
science laid the found-
ation of the practical
successes which created
the industrial revolution

...reaks through the medieval framework

Catalogue No. E.205

(actual size 30″ × 40″)

programmes specially for different age-groups of children, a discrimination which the ordinary film does not possess. Both the B.B.C. and I.T.V. produce a vast range of history broadcasts for children of all ages. The B.B.C., for instance, has had an excellent series on *Exploration and Discovery* for the 10–13 age group, and another for the adolescent on British social history. It has begun a new series, *Out of the Past*, which will be repeated in subsequent years, with programmes revised as necessary. I.T.V. has broadcast *How We used to Live*, produced by Yorkshire Television for children of nine to twelve, a series showing how people have dealt with the various basic problems of life, such as keeping warm, and nursing the sick, through the ages. These programmes are produced by people with a considerable knowledge of the schools and of current educational thinking. They take care to keep in touch with teachers and are always glad of helpful criticism and suggestions. This is clear from the pamphlets which the B.B.C. sends round describing schools broadcasts. A paragraph from the descripton of *Exploration and Discovery* reads: 'This new series tells the story of real events which affect Man's increasing mastery over his environment and which have some inspirational quality for children. It could provide a particuarly valuable contribution to work planned on "integrated" lines and involving an element of team teaching . . . the topics will be chosen to encourage a wide variety of children's research and creative work.'

Considerable help is given to the teacher both by the B.B.C. and by I.T.V., and here again this gives the television companies the advantage over the commercial enterprise producing educational films. If one intends to use programmes, it is advisable to write for information in the summer before the school year begins, or possibly earlier. The Education Officer of the local I.T.V. programme company will provide information about educational programmes; the B.B.C. sends its annual programme for the coming school year to every school in March, and this gives full details of the aims of each series and the nature of the publications which accompany it. Extra copies can be obtained by writing to the School Broadcasting Council for the United Kingdom (30/BC) (see page 154). The teachers' notes and pupils' pamphlets produced by both the B.B.C. and I.T.V. are of a high standard; the material for the children will include vivid pictures and suggestions for many things to do, and these little booklets are well worth keeping as reference books. The teachers' notes will contain suggestions on how to prepare the children for the broadcast and how to follow it up in an interesting way.

It is clear that television companies are well aware of the needs of schools, and many of their programmes are excellent. There is sometimes the disadvantage that times of broadcasts do not fit in with the school timetable; it is possible to overcome this if the school possesses a video-recorder, but not many do. Another problem is that the series may not fit in with the teaching already planned, or with the school syllabus. Most television series are 'line of development' studies stretching over a great length of time, and not all teachers will wish to work in this way. This is a basic drawback to schools television, and the only solution at the moment seems to be to reach a decision on whether the programmes are so good in themselves (and many of them are) as to make it worth while to rearrange the work of the children around them.

In the future there may be other ways of solving these difficulties. The B.B.C. makes available both for purchase and for hire a considerable number of its general service and its educational television programmes. The purchase and hire catalogues come from B.B.C. Television Enterprises (see page 154).

It may be that we shall see a revolutionary change in television broadcasting within the next few years. Television companies have considered making programmes available for redistribution in cassette form. When applied to schools broadcasting, cassette television may well solve the problems of using these programmes in the history lesson. There is also the possibility that material from a television series may appear as a commercially published book. Thames Television's series *Treasures of the British Museum*, in which distinguished men and women, experts in their fields, talked about some of the priceless objects in various departments, has been published in book form by Collins, and the publishers John Murray have issued a book based on Lord Clark's very successful B.B.C. series *Civilisation*.

Audio-visual aids are often put together and talked about as if they were one, but in fact the audio and the visual aid are quite different. The audio aid relies upon the evocativeness of the spoken word, or of sound itself. The word or sound is abstracted from the sensuous impressions that would normally accompany it; if one is listening to an imaginative reconstruction of the past, one might hear the sounds of David Livingstone struggling through the African jungle, but not see him, nor smell the vegetation, nor feel the humidity of the air. This apparent deficiency of the audio aid is, at the same time, its great strength, for it leaves the mind free to conjure up its own images, and these images are peculiarly the individual's. Its very abstract quality, then, makes sound a more adaptable medium than vision. Also, because it relies heavily on the spoken word, the audio aid is a much more efficient way than the visual aid of developing concepts that can only be developed in terms of language, many of which form part of historical thinking.

In accordance with its more abstract nature, the audio aid has one deficiency in that it cannot bring an actual concrete experience into the class-room. With the aid of a picture or film, children can see objects and sometimes events of the past, but they cannot be given this first-hand experience through sound, unless one is playing the music or some of the speeches of the past. In my view, this is more than atoned for in teaching by the way in which the medium leaves the mind free to do its own individual thinking. This can actually be seen in the class-room. A few years back, I played a dramatic reconstruction of the past to some children and then asked them to draw and paint some of the characters whose exploits they had been listening to. The children's drawings showed a vast range. Each child had clearly formed quite different mental images from those of his or her neighbour. This could not have been the case had they been shown actual pictures. Much more research is needed here. When is it better to use an audio rather than a visual aid, or vice versa? Is it better to use one kind of aid rather than the other with children of varying degrees of intelligence? One suspects that research would reveal that highly intelligent children would use the audio aid more efficiently.

Sound is used in various ways as an aid to learning. It can be used to give a straightforward lecture on a subject by an authority one would not perhaps otherwise be able to hear, like Sir Mortimer Wheeler on archaeology, and Glyn Daniel on the origins of civilisation. Or sound can be used as a means of dramatically reconstructing the past, using actors and sound effects. Often the two are combined.

The B.B.C. sound broadcast is by far the most well-known and frequently used audio aid in the schools. There is a vast range of programmes, suitable for children of all ages. The series for one year includes a study of 'Man' for the 10–11 year olds. This is a continuing series, beginning with Man's evolution in the autumn term and then proceeding in the spring to various aspects of his existence, such as *Man the Inventor* and *Living Together*. The summer term is devoted to a study of two particular societies, the Bushmen and the Indian village. Then there is *History in Evidence* (also a continuing series) for the slightly older child (11–14 years), portraying six patches of history from the later days of Roman Britain to the Black Hole of Calcutta and the Boston Tea Party. A resource folder is available for children to use with this series, containing facsimile documentary and visual material. For the 13–16 year olds there is *History in Focus* on themes of modern history; it can be accompanied by radio-vision film-strips. A resource pamphlet is provided.

At junior school level there is *History: Not So Long Ago* (ages 8–11 years), a continuing series on a two-year cycle, starting in the pupils' own lifetime; it will go further back into the past, using a 'patch' approach, from 1974–5. For the middle school and lower secondary pupils (ages 11–12), there is a continuing series starting in 1973–4 with two units, 1: Roman Studies, and 2: An African Casebook. For all these programmes, children's and teachers' materials can be ordered from the School Broadcasting Council for the United Kingdom (see page 154), as for television broadcasts.

One can pick out various trends in B.B.C. broadcasting for schools. The imaginary recreated scene is still very popular, but in addition has come more use of documentary reconstruction, emphasis on local history and the environment, the integrated study based on places and people, and considerable emphasis on problem solving: that is, presenting evidence to children in the form of original sources and allowing them to draw their own conclusions. One must congratulate the B.B.C. on the way its producers keep up with the times. A word of warning to its scriptwriters, though. They should remember that their audiences are accustomed to the dialogue of 'Z-Cars', 'Peyton Place', and James Bond. In the schools broadcasts, some of the dialogue, particularly that between children, has a certain prissiness that makes one suspect that the writers have not been in contact with children for some time.

As with television, there is the problem of incorporating the history broadcast into the work of the class. One solution is to tape-record the programmes, so that they can be used whenever one wants them. The B.B.C. permits this to be done, provided the recording is wiped off after a year (this may soon be extended to two). The alternative is to buy a recording of the broadcast from Stagesound (London) Ltd (see page 153). The recordings (from Radio 4 only) mostly have a limited life expectancy (about one year, or three years for radio-vision), and each costs in the region of £3.

Some years ago a group of London teachers got together in order to exploit the uses of the tape-recorder in the class-room. Since then, led by one of the Inner London Inspectorate, they have produced a variety of tape-recordings on most subjects. So far as history is concerned, there is the 'Blue Plaque' series, which explores the lives of some of the famous people whose former homes in London are distinguished by a blue plaque. Then there is a series of dramatic history plays for the class-room on such subjects as 'The Coming of the Railways' and 'The Suffragettes'. These recordings may be borrowed without charge by any school in the London area on application to 'London Tape' (see page 153). The secretary is always pleased to send out information. Local groups of teachers have many advantages over national organisations, for they understand the needs and interests of their own children and can cater exactly for them. One should also look for ways in which children themselves can use the tape-recorder creatively. Harrap have produced a book of historical plays for children to act and record. It is called *Plays for Reading and Recording*, by S. Love and W. D. Cumming. It would be even better for children to write or improvise their own productions in class, and so find for themselves an exciting new way of learning history.

The music of a people can express its very soul more poignantly than any

Using a BBC taped history programme and support material

other medium. By this I mean, not the classical music of an age, but its folk song, for it is this that expresses the memories, the sufferings and the hopes of a people. There is a revival of interest in folk-song at this very moment, and it is a particularly valuable aid to the teaching of history, for when in the past most people were unable to read or write, when they had few amusements other than those they could make for themselves, and when they experienced a hopelessness that most of us nowadays escape, they sang about their lives. Topic Records Ltd (see page 153) are now reviving this age-old form of music-making and reproducing folk-song in record form. The songs are drawn from the peoples of many countries, Canada, South America, Albania, as well as Britain. Taking one or two titles from British history, 'The Factory Girl', 'The Recruiting Sergeant', 'Pity the Downtrodden Landlord', one can feel the vivid sense of the past which they convey. And how well 'Down on the Picket Line' and 'I hate the Company Bosses' express the bitterness of the Great Depression in America! These songs are not sung in self-consciously artistic style but simply, as the people of the past must have sung them as they went about their daily lives. One word of advice, though, about the use of these records in the class-room: the actual words of the songs cannot always be heard very clearly, and as these are a most valuable resource in the history lesson it is as well to listen to the records yourself first and to copy out the words for the children.

Great events, and particularly the moments of crisis in a nation's history, are often conveyed in the speeches of famous men, or through eye-witness accounts of the people who lived through these times. The Longman Group produces long-playing records in its *Modern Times* series, consisting of eye-witness accounts of dramatic events in twentieth century history, such as the outbreak of World War I, the rise of Hitler, and the making of the Welfare State. Decca has put out selections from the speeches of Winston Churchill; B.B.C. Records has a limited amount of archive material available (see page 153). Audio aids can bring to children some of the original sources of the past.

Recently, another trend has been apparent, and that is to record lectures by well-known authorities on certain subjects for use in schools. In this way children, particularly older children, can hear men and women who are up to the minute in their research and thinking. Discourses Ltd (see page 153) is producing a series of recorded lectures, the first two being A. J. P. Taylor on the Bolshevik Revolution and on Chamberlain and Munich. Educational Audio-Visual Ltd (see page 153) produces sets of coloured film-strips and correlated records on European history, covering such subjects as the French Revolution and the causes of World War I.

One of the latest ventures in this field is Sussex Tapes, distributed by Educational Productions Ltd (see page 153). Two graduates of Sussex University have persuaded various eminent historians to set down their thoughts on tape. One may hear Professor G. R. Elton on the politics of Henry VIII, Dr Christopher Hill on Oliver Cromwell, and Lady Antonia Fraser on Mary,

Queen of Scots. The lectures and discussions on these tape-recordings are suitable for sixth-formers and they are a valuable enrichment of the history lesson. There is something here to ponder over, though. I played one of these tapes to a group of students, and one of them remarked that it was much harder to listen to a taped lecture than to read an article or to listen to a speaker. After some discussion the reason became clear. With a recorded lecture, the listener has to follow at the speaker's pace, he cannot pause or go over a sentence again. Unless the lecture is exactly tuned to the audience, the result may be a hazy impression rather than an accurate intellectual grasp of the subject. It seems, also, that the spoken word loses something through being divorced from its speaker. The gestures, facial expressions and mannerisms of a speaker are a form of communication with his audience that lends much greater depth to what he is saying. It seems that the spoken word cannot really be divorced from the person who is speaking it.

Probably enough has now been said to show that audio-visual aids have an invaluable part to play in the history lesson. I wish, however, to end this chapter with a plea for seeing them in a new perspective, a plea for their more creative use. So often the picture, film, or tape-recording is brought along by the teacher, or the broadcast is used, as a pleasant alternative to his or her own voice. The children sit and watch, or listen. If, however, audio-visual aids were used with more imagination they could bring about a revolution in the class-room. They could be used to create self-motivated learning situations, in which the children themselves use these aids as part of the learning process. The tape-recorder and the film-strip projector are easy for children to use, in fact they often pick up their intricacies far more quickly than the teacher, and simple books are now being written on the use of these aids, both for children and teachers. I am sure that the day is not far off when simple kits will be available for children to produce their own films. It seems to me that the importance of such activity goes far beyond the class-room. We are fond of referring to ourselves as living in a technological society, and yet we distrust technology. One sees this in everyday terms in the number of people, both men and women, who will proudly confess that they are 'hopeless' with anything mechanical. We express our fear in philosophical terms when we cry that men are becoming the slaves of technological progress, or, more subtly, when we say that man has progressed materially, but not morally. We are really putting into words the nightmare that we can no longer control our technological environment. One cannot help feeling that many of these fears, this feeling of inadequacy, would disappear if children were accustomed to handle machinery, to seeing it as a natural means of self-expression, from an early age, in much the same way as they learn to handle words. Frequent familiarity could teach children that technology is an ally, that it can be part of their way of thinking and actually bring about a richer way of life. Who knows? The creative use of audio-visual aids in the class-room may one day bring about a happier society.

6

The Teaching of History and the Organisation of the Class

Twenty years ago there was only one way of organising the class for the teaching of history, or of anything else. The children sat in straight rows, in silence, of course, and the teacher faced them and addressed them. After such an address, or perhaps the reading aloud of a chapter from a book, the class set to and wrote what they had heard, memorising the content. The success of the lesson was judged by the amount the children had remembered.

Nowadays the picture is very different. There has been a great deal of educational re-thinking, and of thinking about the child himself. There has emerged a more sensitive attitude to the child and the way in which he learns, so that there is now a whole range of activities within the class-room. The traditional school subjects, of which history is one, have not always kept pace with these activities. In particular there is the problem of how to organise the class for this new kind of teaching. When should children work in groups, for example, and how is group activity best organised? What should one expect of it? Do all children profit equally from individual project work? Above all, what is the role of the teacher when the class is engaged in these various activities? This last point bothers many teachers, for often we do not quite know where we are, or what our role should be. Indeed, with the current emphasis on child-centred learning, the teacher sometimes feels superfluous, and has a guilty feeling that he need not be there at all. Some of these questions, and their relationship to the teaching of history today, will be discussed in this chapter.

The first point to be considered is the nature of the class that the teacher of history invariably meets. It is invariably unstreamed. This has always applied to younger children; now it is increasingly the case with older children also. The trend in secondary schools is, at this moment, towards the unstreamed class. Even when children are setted for subjects like mathematics and languages, they are rarely setted for history. The outstanding feature of history teaching today is that it is carried out in classes of children of mixed ability. This means that the average history teacher customarily faces a group of forty or more children with a considerable range of intelligence, not to say interests. He is aware of this divergence and also of the acceptance that each child must work to his own capacity and be taught as an individual. How then can he teach them?

There are various ways of organising the class in the history lesson. Each has a different end, and in each the role of the teacher varies. These differences apply, not only to the intellectual relationship in which the teacher stands to the class, but also to his psychological role. When one kind of activity is engaged upon, he may be the figure of authority, the taker of intiative; in another activity, he may slide quietly into the background, leaving the initiative to the children. Above all, the history teacher today must be aware of the needs of his class and be able to adapt himself swiftly and sensitively.

The simplest kind of class organisation is when the class as a unit faces the teacher. 'Faces' is perhaps too strong a word, implying as it does some kind of battle, but at any rate it signifies the one-to-one relationship that is the essence of this grouping. This kind of organisation is appropriate when the teacher has something to say or do that concerns all the children in the class equally, whatever their differences in ability and interests. He or she may be giving a talk on a certain subject, or leading a discussion, or perhaps acting as a catalyst and stimulating the children to awareness and interest. I know of a teacher who once rushed into a class-room splendidly dressed as a cavalier. He was going to give a talk on the English Civil War and intended to capture everyone's attention. He certainly did. The teacher, when he accepts this kind of role in relationship to his class, is being much more than the mere purveyor of information, even when he is talking history. He represents the adult world, with the status and modes of action and thought that the children may one day adopt themselves. The importance of adults to children is now very much played down, it being sometimes accepted that the children have their existence, the adults theirs, and that the two can never meet. However, the two worlds can meet; in fact, they must meet if children are to grow up. Children themselves are keenly aware of this, and there is nothing they appreciate more than contact with their teacher, so that it is a great thing to be able to talk freely and frankly with one's class, being oneself, whether in a history or in any other kind of lesson.

One should also be aware that the relationship of teacher to class carries over to those activities when the children are apparently working by themselves. They may be listening to a broadcast or writing individual assignments, but what they do and how they do it is greatly influenced by their relationship with their teacher. If this is good and creative, the children's work invariably is also.

Of the two relationships essential to the boy or girl in the class-room, one is with his teacher and the other is with the rest of the children. Another psychological role of great importance that the teacher plays out in this one-to-one relationship with the class is that of drawing it together into a community. His is a unique position, because only he is outside the class. It is difficult to explain in theoretical terms the effect the community feeling of a class has on its individual members, but any practising teacher knows that this is vital. Every individual, child or adult, needs to be of value to, and to have a place in, a large community. Otherwise he or she becomes disorientated and unable to work. This may seem a far cry from the teaching of history, but the teacher of history, when he is talking to his class as a whole, whatever his topic, is addressing them as one. Apart from this, in the responses he calls for from various members, and the way in which he knits them into the lesson, the good teacher makes his children feel both part of the activity and of the group. His relationship with the children is a vital factor in their relationship with each other.

The unit organisation of the class is widely used today, especially with older children. Although the teacher on these occasions seems to be the active one, the children should be just as active in the intellectual sense, and should be working just as hard. They will need time to themselves afterwards, in order to consolidate what they have heard. A teacher should never talk too long to a class. With young children, who cannot concentrate for long, a story or talk should rarely last longer than about fifteen minutes. Older children can listen for much longer periods, of up to an hour.

Very relevant to the teaching of history is the organisation of the class into groups. It is interesting to consider what exactly a group is. One characteristic is easy to see, and that is that it consists of children working with one another. Most usually they are working with children of their own age; occasionally they are put together with others of similar ability, as is often the case with subjects like reading and number, but hardly ever in the case of a subject of supposedly general interest like history. In infant schools, the children may also work in family groupings, that is, in groups containing children of various ages, just as one would expect to find in a family. Family grouping is hardly ever tried with older children, though one cannot help feeling it would be an interesting experiment.

There are various ways of grouping the children. There is the peer group, which is the group of equals in age; there is the ability group, where the children fall within a certain range of ability; and there is the family group, and lastly the friendship group. Groupings also differ according to whether they are chosen by the teacher or by the children themselves.

There is, however, another important characteristic of the group, and that is that its members feel themselves to be a community. After all, one could call a class of forty children a group, but one would hardly do so in our sense, and the reason reflects an interesting psychological fact. The individual, and this applies to adults as well as children, can only form emotional ties with a limited number of people. Children show themselves to be very well aware of this. When asked to form themselves into groups, after a few minutes of chaos

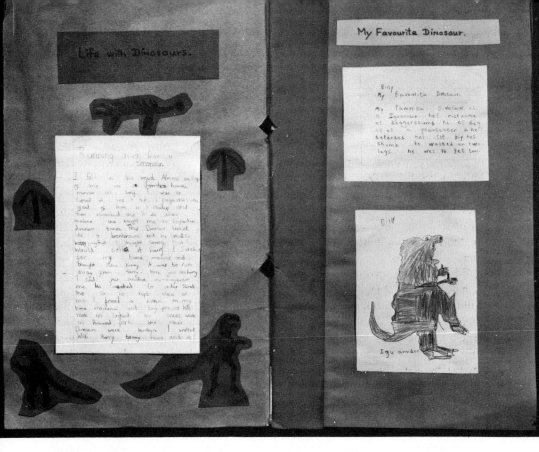

From a book on dinosaurs, made by a group of nine-year-olds

they commonly form into groups of between three and six. With fewer than three, the relationship is too close for the work they have to do; with more than six the bond is not strong enough. Ease of communication plays its part too. Group organisation, then, implies the feeling that the members of the group belong to each other, this feeling being expressed in a certain range of membership. It also implies a common aim.

What kind of group organisation is the most relevant to the teaching of history today? I suggest that the most valuable is the broadly based grouping, chosen by the children themselves, without bothering about streaming within the class. I believe this both because of the nature of history as a subject and on general educational grounds. History is a cultural subject, with an enormous appeal to children of all ages and abilities. It does not depend on any one specific aptitude, or on any special technique. It makes possible many different ways of working and calls for many talents. This being the case, it is relevant, even harmful, to group children narrowly according to measured intelligence. In actual fact, there is less of a contrast between the two forms of grouping than one might imagine, for children, left to themselves, nearly always choose equals or near-equals in ability with whom to work.

On general educational grounds, one of the most valuable assets of group work is that it frees the children from the teacher. This remark may seem strange, when the importance of the teacher has just been stressed, but the truth is that it is just as important for children occasionally to work with each other as it is for them to work with a teacher. Grouping gives them this opportunity of activity in a situation they themselves have created, but it is only successful if they are allowed to choose the grouping. Children know instinctively with whom they wish to work, just as adults do. Left alone, they form their own little community, with its own rules, its own leaders and its own discipline adapted to the common task. They should be left freely in this children's world, for in it they learn lessons that adults cannot teach them.

What can the group organisation of the class add to the history lesson? It has, firstly, valuable contributions to make to the social development of children, and these apply whatever the subject being studied. Members of a group come to understand one another's strengths and weaknesses; they accept a discipline in order to achieve a common end, and the group relationship is able often to contain the aggressive or lazy child more effectively than the teacher can. These are valuable social lessons, by no means divorced from intellectual achievement, for mental effort is closely conditioned by the social milieu. The co-operative way of working is also in many ways the most natural to children. We may live in a highly competitive society, but children give many indications, especially in the happiness they show when engaged in co-operative work, that this is the way that comes most naturally to them. Group activity has other merits. It can often give the less able or uneasy child an added sense of security, and even on a purely intellectual plane children can sometimes clear up one another's difficulties in a remarkably short time.

More specifically, the group organisation of the class leads itself to various kinds of activity in the history lessons. It is most appropriate when a common end can be set, and when the achievement of this end calls for various abilities. This is usually the case when a group of children is engaged on practical work, such as a model. Planning and preparing this kind of work has already been discussed in the chapter on the creative approach. It is also appropriate in the 'patch' or 'line of development' study, when several children work together to produce a detailed account of one period or one development in historical time. Dramatic work, and the playing of games, two interesting approaches to the teaching of history, are also appropriate. In fact, without grouping they cannot be carried out at all.

Group work is also particularly applicable to certain children. It can give reassurance to the backward or insecure; it is also greatly enjoyed by boys and girls in the seven to twelve age range, who happen to be at a stage in development when they prefer to be continually in each other's company.

However, one ought also to consider whether there is any activity that is appropriate to the group, particularly as group work is currently so fashionable and therefore deserves especially hard scrutiny. One kind of work can never be done in a group and that is truly creative work. This is always produced by one person working alone. No great poem, book or painting is ever produced by a team. It is true that individuals can collaborate in the writing of a book or the painting of a picture, but only when scope is given within the broad aim for the artists to work according to their unique and personal vision. Therefore I would hold that it is quite inappropriate to ask a group of children to produce something as intensely personal and creative as an essay, or a poem. Children will gladly work together to write and produce a drama, but in fact they invariably allot the actual writing to one member of the group. It is the case that a high intellectual standard, in the academic sense, is rarely achieved by group work, probably because work at this level is an intensely personal matter.

Neither is group activity equally appropriate to all kinds of children. The extremely able child, and the creative child, will often prefer to work by him- or herself, and should be allowed to do so. Again, this kind of activity is very popular with young children, but much less so with the adolescent, whose interest and abilities are by now so highly developed as to make him much more individualistic. For these reasons, the group organisation of the class should not be adopted all the time, nor with all children.

There are two forms of group work which deserve to be discussed in detail, as both have considerable, though sometimes overlooked, value in the teaching of history. The first of these is dramatic work. Drama involves essentially the projection of oneself into another situation and a different role. The actor is, for the time being, someone else. This is peculiarly relevant to an imaginative understanding of the past, for in thinking himself into the role of a person from another age, the child reconstructs it. For those who insist that the efficiency of any method of teaching should be judged by how many facts can be remembered, it is worth remarking that the child who has acted out something of the life of a person from history rarely forgets it, and seems to receive the inspiration to seek out more knowledge in the factual sense, associating that person, as he does, with his own identity.

Role-playing has great appeal for young children, for it gives them the opportunity for identifying and finding themselves, at the very moment when they need this experience. Drama is also well-tailored to the child's love of excitement, for the skeleton of drama is action, with no description and little introspection, so that it seems a natural mode of expression for him. The writing, producing and acting out of a play, calling as it does for a whole range of activities, and then for an audience to appreciate the finished product, is ideal for group-work in the class-room. Drama is, in a sense, real life stripped to its bare bones, with all the qualities of impact and immediacy that that implies, and it is a pity that it is not more used in the history lesson. Longman has published *Four Plays from History* by Kenneth Nuttall, covering the Roman withdrawal from Britain, the travels of Marco Polo, the voyage of the *Mayflower*, and the suffragette movement.

Better still, the children can create their own drama. If they are working in groups, they readily assign the writing to those members with a flair for it, while the others proceed with the business of props and production. Young children often like to dramatise an incident impromptu. Props are not really necessary for the class-room drama; it can even be argued that they inhibit the imaginative effort one hopes to encourage. However, many teachers find that a few props of a symbolic nature, like a crown to symbolise kingship and a sword to represent fighting, are appreciated by the children and add glamour to the occasion.

At first sight, the playing of games in the history lesson seems a far cry from drama, but in fact the two have several qualities in common. Both are vivid, both are 'real' in a sense that the child appreciates, and both lend themselves to group organisation. The playing of games is at once a very old and a very new approach. Increasingly, in recent years, it has become more and more popular as an educational method for all kinds of subjects. It is just beginning to gain a new foothold in schools and colleges. There are sound educational reasons for this growing popularity, for children are inveterate games-players. Games seem to be the one activity they are always ready for. Left for a moment to their own devices, within minutes they are playing a game—marbles, or conkers, 'He', riddles, or word-games. If nobody has a game handy, somebody speedily invents one. Their love of games frequently lands children in trouble, for it is assumed by many to run counter to the sober processes of learning, and to be an enemy that must be routed as soon as it peeps round the class-room door. Instead, perhaps we should ask ourselves why it is that games have this perennial fascination for children, and how we can make use of it in the class-room.

We might consider first why games are so popular. To help in this, think about that old favourite, 'Snakes and Ladders'.

All games, of whatever kind, have certain characteristics in common, where-in lie their appeal. Their outstanding characteristic is that they are invariably competitive. In conkers, it is one conker against another; in riddles, so much loved by children between the ages of seven and eleven, it is one person's verbal ingenuity against another's; in 'Snakes and Ladders' it is two or more counters competing against each other in order to reach 'home' first. Often, as in team games, there is a strong element of co-operation as well. This not only gives the competitior the comfort of belonging to a group, but actually increases the competitive element, for the stakes are that much higher.

Secondly, all games have in them an element of chance, or luck. In 'Snakes and Ladders', and many games like it, luck is represented by the dice; in card games, it is represented by the fall of the card; in athletic activities, such as rounders and football, luck is seen in the trip of the fielder as he runs for the catch, or in the rebound of the ball as it hits the goalpost. Luck, like competition, is part of life, the unforseen that waits for us all around the corner beyond human control. In some games, though, the player is given the opportunity of out-witting luck. He does this either by the adaptability and intelligence he shows in decision-making, as in Monopoly, or by his physical endurance and skill, as in field games. This, again, is life writ on a smaller scale.

There is also in games a strong element of fantasy. The exact degree of this fantasy is a debatable point, but it exists in most games. Fantasy is the playing out of action on two levels at the same time, the conscious and the subconscious. There are those who are quick to point out the sexual fantasy implied in the playing of football, and even in the seemingly innocent 'Snakes and Ladders'. While one does not have to subscribe completely to this view, the fascination that certain games possess, even to the point of obsession, certainly seems to point to the existence of a double-action, to a significance beyond the obvious one. It does not have to be sexual; the player can be outwardly playing 'Snakes and Ladders', moving his counters along, but inwardly reassuring himself that he too can overcome difficulties, that he too has luck on his side. This would surely explain the fascination that many games have for young children, for it is between the ages of five and twelve, in the middle years, that they live this intensely inner life.

Another characteristic of games greatly appeals to children. It is that they are usually crude. By this I mean that the issues are simple and always expressed in outward action. This is what makes games exciting and dramatic. This characteristic is obvious in those that involve physical action; in those in which physical action plays less part this crudeness is expressed in the existence of very bright colours. Can anyone imagine a Ludo game printed in subtle shades of mauve, brown and greens?

The attraction of games can be summed up by saying that they mirror life, but safely and on a smaller time and space scale. They have a particular appeal for children because they fulfil their psychological needs. How, then, can they be adapted to the history lesson?

There are two kinds of educational game; the role-playing game, in which the participants are encouraged to make the right decisions and so win, and the game that is merely descriptive. The role-playing game is increasingly the vogue in America, where it is used as a teaching method quite outside the schools. It is used in business schools, for example, as a means of training business executives to assess economic situations efficiently. I would like to discuss the role-playing game first, partly because, in common with many of my colleagues, I am not altogether happy about its use with children.

In 1971 Francis Hill reported in *The Times Educational Supplement* (15 January 1971) on an American game called 'Star-power'. This aims at modifying the player's social and racial attitudes in the following way. The class is divided into three groups consisting of squares, circles and triangles and each team is given counters with which they trade. The point is that the squares' counters are worth more than the circles, and the circles' more than the triangles'. This mirrors society, and it is meant to teach children what it is like to be black and poor, or perhaps white and rich, and to provoke discussion on these points. There are many strong advocates of the simulation game as a teaching method in England as well as in America, holding it to involve active participation by the child and to abolish the need for an authoritarian figure in the shape of the teacher. The Society for Academic Games and Simulations in Education and Training, 5 Errington, Moreton-in-Marsh, Glos., runs regular courses for teachers, including teachers of history, on various ways of teaching by means of role-playing games. However, many people have grave doubts about this kind of game. It is by no means proven that the child can bridge the gap between the game and reality, and carry the lesson learnt over into real life. It also seems a clumsy and crude way of reconstructing any historical situation, differing as this must do from our own situation in so many different ways. More seriously, many teachers are suspicious of anything that seeks to mould or motivate a child by means of which he is unaware. Some would much prefer, if children's attitudes need to be changed, to change them by frank and open discussion.

Just because some simulation games seek to change attitudes, there is in them, in my view, an assumption that runs counter to modern educational thinking. They are essentially authoritarian and assume that the teacher's attitudes are right. There is no guarantee of this, even though it may seem so at the time. Further, true education can take place only on the assumption that teacher and taught, given the obvious differences in knowledge and maturity, are essentially equals. It cannot proceed on any other basis. The simulation and role-playing games, then, should come under the very close scrutiny of the teacher before they are allowed in the class-room.

The descriptive game is another matter. It aims simply at describing a situation to the children, who then participate in it by playing the game. It can also be an attractive way of introducing children to certain historical facts that one is anxious for them to remember. Inventing games for one's class to play in groups can be a fascinating and by no means difficult pastime. The first essential in devising such a game is to have in mind a specific situation. Let us suppose we are setting out to portray what it was like to cross the seas in mediaeval times. We can call it 'A Voyage across the Ocean in the Middle Ages', and it can be simply based on those dice-throwing and counter-moving games that children love, of which 'Ludo' and 'Snakes and Ladders' are just two.

In mediaeval times, when seamen lacked the knowledge and equipment they have today, a long sea journey was fraught with danger. The ships themselves were small and, because they ran under sail, were at the mercy of wind and current. There was the problem of disease, contributed to by faulty diet; there was the threat of mutiny by the crew, and the possibility of getting lost when out of sight of land; worst of all, there lurked in every seaman's mind the fear of horrible sea-monsters. There were no lighthouses or buoys to warn these tiny ships of the danger of rocks or current. Against these perils the captain and crew pitted their skill and determination aided, they hoped, by good fortune. It is a situation that can easily be translated into a game. A diagram of one version is seen opposite. Played with dice and counters, the only point to remember is that each player must be given the same number of misfortunes and also the same degree of good luck as all the others.

By the time a group of children had played this game several times, they would know something of the hazards of mediaeval seamanship. Games can be readily adapted to all kinds of historical situations, and every teacher will have his or her own ideas. It is a good plan to watch the games that children are playing of their own accord, and to base one's own historical game on that. This is amusing for the children as well as the teacher. It would certainly be possible to devise a historical game based on 'He' or 'Tag'.

The playing of games, then, is another activity that can be introduced to advantage when the teacher wishes to adapt the group organisation of the class. It is often a good method for those children whom the teacher wishes to remember a limited amount of information well, such as very young or backward children.

There are, however, in spite of the attractions, certain limitations to the playing of games that should be borne in mind. Older children do not take to games as readily as younger ones, and games can portray certain aspects of history only. These are essentially descriptive. It is much more difficult to devise games that show the relationship between cause and effect, or which deal with an abstract subject. There is, lastly, the ever-present danger that games-playing may descend into gimickry. It is worth remembering that if a subject has to be tricked out too much in order to make it palatable then one should not be teaching it.

Games-playing, historical studies in depth, drama and practical work are all appropriate to group organisation in the history lesson. What should the role of the teacher be? It is certainly quite different, and not nearly so clear-cut, as when he is dealing with the class as a whole, talking to them, say, or showing them a film. Nevertheless, he has a vital role to play, in helping to decide the end to which group-work is directed, in assisting while it is actually proceeding, and in bringing about its successful conclusion.

The teacher takes the initiative in deciding what the end of group activity shall be. I say 'take the initiative' because in truth the kind of work to be done is actually divided jointly between teacher and children. If the children appear to do the choosing, their choice will be conditioned by the teaching that has gone before; if the teacher does the choosing he will instinctively choose something that he knows will be appropriate. A typical example would be when the children have been studying, say, prehistory, and the teacher suggests that each group makes a model portraying an era of its choice. In this way the groups are given freedom of choice within a broad framework.

The membership of groups and the organisation within them should be left to the children. Some teachers organise each group down to the last detail, as well as allotting the children, even instructing one child to make all the dinosaurs and another to make all the ferns. This is a bad practice educationally. The reason is that what results is not a group but a kind of random coupling; the children will find it difficult to work together and will not form a real community. It is in the nature of group membership to be self-determined so the teacher should respect this.

Sometimes, allowing the children their freedom in this way brings apparent problems. Some children cannot cope with a group relationship, or are reluctant to do so. There is the natural lone wolf, often a boy or girl of distinctive ability, who would rather work by himself. There is the child who clings to the teacher, lacking as yet the maturity with which to cope with his peers, and preferring a parent figure. Sometimes a pair of children will insist on working together, feeling their own close relationship to exclude any wider one. All these children have to be helped. The teacher must find ways of including them in the general scheme while allowing them to work in their own way, for they make it clear that they cannot meet the demands of the group. More distressing can be the outcast, the child whom no group will accept, though he himself is anxious to be included. The reasons for this are usually complex, but it is useless to try to force a group to accept him. The teacher has to look after him, giving him something attractive to do by himself, so that he too ends with a feeling of achievement.

It is the role of the teacher, in his maturity, to sort these problems out. He also exerts an important influence on the work of the groups while it is actually going on. This influence on the way in which children co-operate exerts itself long before the groups begin their activity. It is a humbling truth that children rarely work happily among themselves unless their relationship with their teacher is a good one. That is why it is no use seeking a refuge in this kind of activity if one's class is unmanageable; it will be even worse when organised in groups. It is also the reason why the teacher whose class appears capable of working without him has cause only to congratulate himself. He has forged a happy community.

Not only does he exert a vital if unseen influence on the way in which the groups set about their work, the teacher also has clear cut duties in providing the background for their activity. He has, firstly, to provide the right class-room environment. This means, in the case of practical work, seeing that a plentiful supply of stimulating material is at hand. (This was fully discussed in the chapter on the creative approach.) In the case of a 'patch' or special study involving the use of books, these must be suitable and easily accessible. This may involve a complete rearrangement of the class-room. Sometimes

Board game : a voyage across the ocean in mediaeval times
(short version)

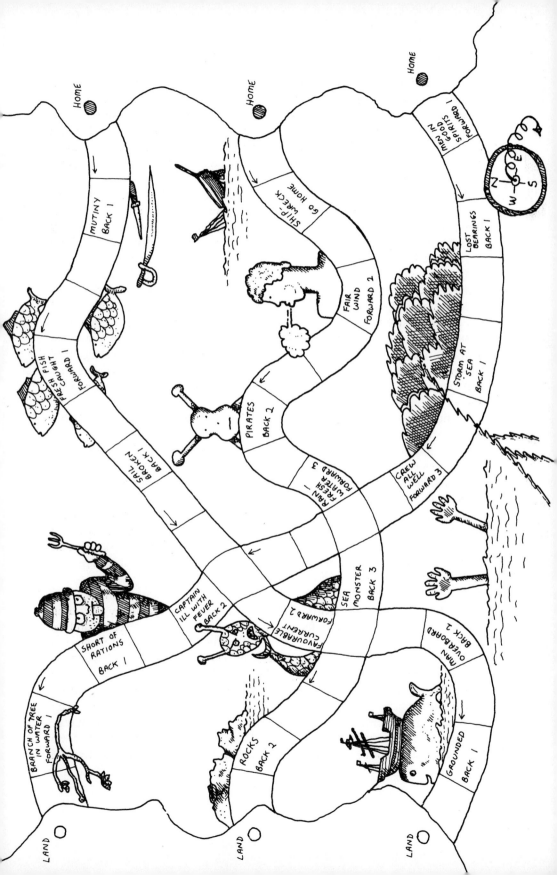

group organisation is used to produce a 'patch' study of a historical period, such as Tudor England, with each group working on one aspect. In this case, the teacher has the vital role of co-ordinator. He must make sure that each group does, in fact, present its findings to the rest of the class, otherwise the children will only know about the particular aspect they have studied. Similarly, it is for the teacher to allot the time available for the work in hand, for only he can know how long this is likely to be.

The teacher must undertake all this when the children are working in groups, for the simple reason that he occupies a unique position. Only he has the experience, the knowledge of the subject, and the advantage of being able to survey the activity without being actually involved in it, that these decisions call for. The children cannot make them for themselves.

In other respects, the children need to call upon the maturity and under-standing of the teacher. There will be numerous occasions when they will call on him to help them out of a difficulty, whether this be a figure in a model which won't stand up, or a word whose meaning defeats them. Such help should be freely given, for the group is calling on the goodwill and superior skill of a friendly adult, as should be the right of all children. It is sometimes forgotten that there is a very simple and effective way of learning, one that is revered in all primitive societies, and that is to be shown by someone who knows.

From the children's point of view, perhaps the teacher is most valuable as group activity draws to an end, for it must fall to him to see that the work is brought to a successful conclusion. A big undertaking of this kind is a severe test of discipline and co-operation for children. These qualities de-mand a considerable degree of maturity, which many children will not yet possess; indeed, one of the reasons for giving them this work is to encourage their development. This means that there may well be occasions when a group of children flags; it is then up to the teacher to help them on. Nothing is so dispiriting to a child as to set out to do something and fail to achieve it. Repeated failure is damaging to the personality, especially to the young one, and the teacher should avoid it for his children.

The teacher, then, has a vital part to play the whole time group activity is going on. He helps to decide its end, he makes work possible by providing the right environment, both in a physical and an emotional sense, and he maintains his role of friend and parent-figure for those who need it. Lastly, he can learn a good deal about his children by watching them at work together, in situations of their own creating, and this knowledge will stand him in good stead. It is surprising, sometimes, to see which child emerges as a natural leader—it is scarcely ever the child who appears so capable when safely in an authoritarian climate; it is salutary to see abilities and creativeness emerge in children one would never have thought possessed them. The teacher, no less than the children, has much to learn from the group organisation of the class.

We come now to the third main way in which the class may be organised for the teaching of history. This differs both from the unit and the group organisation of the children, for it is when they work entirely by themselves, being freed from both their teacher and their fellows. This is known as individual project work. Each child is set or chooses an assignment: it may be a piece of written work, a painting, a model, or a piece of historical investigation, which he works on by himself and completes within a given time. The time allotted may vary greatly, from a single lesson to a few weeks, or even half a term.

There are many advantages in this kind of work, the most important being that the child is set completely free to work at his own pace and to follow his own interests. He is not dictated to either by his fellows or by his teacher. For this reason the individual project is very useful among children where there is a wide range of ability; it is one way of surmounting the obstacles of the unstreamed class. Because the child is thrown upon his own resources, this kind of work often develops his personality. Sometimes, one can see a tremendous improvement, not only in intellectual standards, but in behaviour and poise also. I once knew a very difficult girl of thirteen, most of whose spare time was spent on street corners, and whose school work was invariably dirty, thumb-marked and badly produced, who chose to carry out a written project on Shakespeare. More than surprised at her choice, her teachers were astounded to see the result—beautifully written and illustrated, sensitive and thoughtful, an impeccable piece of work. When she was asked, delicately, to explain the contrast with her usual work, she made the humbling reply, 'I liked doing it.' The interesting thing was that she then carried the improvement over into her other work. Somehow, perhaps because she was ready just at that moment, the project had helped her find herself. This can often be the case. It may be so because of the demands such work makes on the individual. He has to be able to organise himself, to work independently, to call upon his inner resources. Such an effort develops him as a person.

Apart from helping to develop a child both intellectually and emotionally, the individual project often demands that he work in as broad a way as possible. He may have to use the library—school or public—to find the answers to the questions he is asking; he may seek the help of parents and friends right outside school, thus integrating the world outside with his schoolwork. Perhaps the most precious attribute of the project is that it enables the individual boy or girl to work creatively. It is very difficult to define exactly what creativity is and even more difficult to subject it to any kind of scientific test. It shows itself in all spheres of life. It seems to be a complex matter, bearing some kind of relationship to intelligence, emotional factors and even social relationships. Recent research tends to suggest that the creative child has had a particular relationship with his mother. One characteristic of creativeness in a person seems clear, and that is that it involves the ability to make something new, to see a new relationship. This new relationship may be seen intellectually, as the historian Namier applied it to the political scene of the eighteenth century; in art and literature it may express itself in an entirely new vision of what life is about, so that when we put down a book or see a painting, we know that we have glimpsed a new world. Some people reveal this quality, not in anything they make, but in the way they live, in a new life-style. However it manifests itself, creativeness is vitally important, and to encourage it should be one of the aims of all teaching. For one thing, creative-ness is a source of great satisfaction and happiness to the individual. For another, it is the individual's contribution towards society, towards the com-munity in which he lives. Only by adapting itself continually can a society survive. The inventor of the flint tool helped his community survive; today we are waiting for creative men and women to solve the problems of pollution, poverty and war, perhaps by seeing these things in an entirely new way. The more quickly society changes—and it is generally accepted that rapid change is in-built in our kind of community—the more vital this quality of creative-ness becomes. We should therefore wish to encourage it in children as much as we can. As creative work, being unique to one person, can only be done by an individual, the well-set project is its natural vehicle. It is significant that it is the able and intelligent child who enjoys this way of working most. Giving children this kind of opportunity in the history lesson, apart from its broader benefits, may result in the making of a new historian.

Great as its benefits may be, though, the individual project as a way of working can present problems. To look at the other side of the picture, al-though the able and creative child may take to it, the dull child may find it unrewarding. It may assume intellectual resources that simply are not there, or a capacity for sustained effort, even for half-an-hour, that is likewise absent. There are some children who, being of limited ability, need the constant stimulation that only the adult with a wider horizon can give them. This method also assumes strong motivation on the part of the child, and we all know the individual who, when asked what he wants to do, replies, 'Nothing.' The essential drawback of the individual project is that it denies children, for the time being, contact with the adult world, so that the less fortunate child may find himself trapped in his own deficiencies. He should not be left there too long. It is also surprising how unpopular this way of working can be with children. There is a school where a groan goes up every time the word 'project' is mentioned, and there was the case where the parents of one school protested to the local Education Officer that their children were continually being set projects. In these cases, one suspects that the method is being abused. Perhaps such work is being demanded of the wrong children, or just doled out irrespective of whether they wish to do it. As project work demands a strong degree of motivation and considerable stamina on the part of the child, it should only be given where these qualities are present. It also needs careful timing, and this is where one suspects many teachers go wrong. Children cannot work too long alone without the stimulus of each other or the teacher. In the case of very young children the time allotted should not be more than a lesson or two; with older children a project can last for up to half a term. It should also be remembered that the project of a practical nature takes longer.

The teacher should maintain contact with the child while he is at work, being at hand to guide him in his research. He should also take care to provide suitable books and materials. So often a child is defeated by being told to 'go to the library', where he tries to wade through books he cannot possibly understand.

While the class is engaged upon individual project work, the teacher still has a vital part to play. His is the skilled task of matching the assignment to the individual child and, once more, of creating the right environment. This is not just a matter of making material provision, but is equally achieved through the relationship he has already forged with the children. If his teaching has been adventurous and stimulating, the desire to strike out by themselves, to stand on their own feet, will almost certainly be there.

I would now like to describe some individual projects carried out by a class of eleven-year-old girls, and to point out some of the characteristics that commonly emerge in this kind of work.

These children had been studying prehistory for two terms. They were then asked to make a special study of any topic they would have liked to have studied more deeply, had there been time. These projects formed part of the annual history examination. It was hoped that they would enable some kind of estimate to be made of such attributes as initiative, depth of research and even aesthetic quality that are not normally revealed in an examination, important though they are. The project was allotted four weeks, during which period the children could use their history lessons (two a week), their history homework allocation, any extra time they chose, on their project. They were allowed to work in whatever manner they pleased, to get help from home or their local library, and to make and bind their own booklets. During the actual lesson times, the teacher was at hand to discuss problems and to point out sources of information if required. She also discussed each child's proposed project with her before she began, to make quite sure that no one was going to embark on a history of the world in thirty pages, as children sometimes do. Another precaution was taken. When the projects were finished, the teacher had another short session with each child, discussing her work and asking her questions about it. This was to make sure that the work really was her own and that she had understood it. All the children knew this before they began. Certain characteristics of this kind of work emerged.

There was a much greater spread of subject matter than one would normally find in a history lesson. Titles ranged across history, geography and science. One child chose a purely scientific subject, genetics, because she said that this was what she was really interested in. Permission to do this was readily granted. This little girl, who produced probably the highest intellectual standard of them all, wanted to be a doctor. She was helped a great deal by her uncle, who was a chemist. The range of titles chosen was far wider than the teacher herself could have thought of, thus proving the value of setting children free to follow their own interests.

There was also a much greater range in the quality of the work than is normally found in the conventional history lesson. The work ranged from a very high intellectual standard, to a very low level. One child produced only four scrappy pages in as many weeks.

The standard of the work seemed related as much to the enthusiasm of the girl concerned as to her intelligence. The best work was not necessarily produced by the brightest children, though this was often the case. This, I think, shows the importance of interest and motivation. There is also a warning implicit here; some children get a good deal less from this kind of work than others.

The children who produced the best work on the whole enjoyed it most, and vice versa. Individuals also showed a high degree of self-awareness. Those whose work was poor were dissatisfied with it and despondent, thus, I think, showing that individual work of this nature heightens self-criticism. These characteristics are apparent whenever a class engages on this kind of work and, I believe, indicate clearly the circumstances in which one should set it.

In closing this discussion on the value of individual project work in the teaching of history, I should like to make a plea for projects of an artistic nature. The history project most frequently set is the one involving a piece of research, or an essay, or the amassing of information. There is a place, too, for the imaginative story, the painting, and even the poem. In reaching out imaginatively, a child can come to understand the past more truly than through memorising facts. Here is a poem that a very backward child of thirteen wrote about King Harold, who was defeated in the Battle of Hastings. Most of her friends chose to write adventure stories about the victorious Normans, but she, with the sensitivity children so often show, felt the pathos of the defeated Saxon king.

> The waves washed over Harold the King
> As he lay on the shore.
> But nobody noticed
> Harold the King,
> As the waves washed over him.

To the three ways of organising the class in the history lesson that have so far been discussed, another has been added in recent years, involving quite a new perspective. This is when the class is involved in an integrated study. In this kind of work subject boundaries are abolished, and the teacher, or sometimes a team of teachers, works across the various disciplines.

The inter-disciplinary approach to learning has become more and more in vogue in recent years, from universities right down to the infant school. In the schools it has sometimes led to history and geography being dispensed with altogether to be replaced by environmental studies for the younger children and usually civics for the older ones. In the universities it has given rise to the introduction of new degree courses involving a grounding in several disciplines. Several factors have contributed to this movement, arising from the nature of knowledge itself and from our increased understanding of how the child thinks and learns.

At first sight, the inter-disciplinary approach seems the only one possible. Knowledge, it can be argued, is one, and it cannot be compartmentalised. If it is, it loses by it and becomes less than itself. Neither, it has been shown, does the child think in compartments, and its interests cannot be channelled into the old-fashioned disciplines without harming it. This reasoning is reinforced by what is taking place in the academic world today, for the actual subject matter of various departments is merging with new disciplines. The geographer, for example, cannot now be content with a knowledge of geography, he has to be something of a scientist and geologist as well, not to say statistician. It is this impingement of one subject on another that has given rise to the new courses in environmental science in the universities.

These developments make the case for the integrated study seem almost inviolable. However, the very factors that are breaking down the barriers between subjects are at the same time working to make them even more rigid. For, as the accumulated knowledge of our society increases and one compartment impinges on another, so also does increased specialisation become inevitable, for no one mind can hold it all. We have now not only the scientist, but the chemist, botanist and physicist, and not only the physicist, but the chemical physicist, the nuclear physicist, and many sub-divisions within these branches of learning that only the specialist can understand. We have not only the historian, but also the economic, the constitutional and the political historian. Economic and social forces are pulling equally strongly away from integration and making for the increasing fragmentation of knowledge. Our economy, and with it our material standard of living, is based on the specialisation of economic function. In the factory, a worker may spend his life pushing one button, squeezing one dab of cream on to a chocolate cake, pulling one lever, over and over again. The same pattern is repeated all the way up the social scale.

In practice, the schools are caught squarely between these opposing trends towards and against the integration of knowledge, and so is the child. He starts his school life with the integrated day and child-centred activities, only to be required, at an increasingly early age, to choose which subjects in which to specialise so that he can get a job when he leaves school.

Nor should other arguments be overlooked when it comes to weighing up the case for and against the integrated study. The arguments of those in favour of dispensing with the boundaries that separate the various academic subjects seem, at first sight, so cogent that one is tempted to ask why these subjects ever came into being in the first place. What is a subject, and what distinguishes it from every other? The numerous disciplines can be seen to differ from one another, firstly in their subject matter. Botany is clearly concerned with plants, music with sound, history with the events and people of the past, and so on. However, in many cases, the same material comes within the sphere of several subjects. A stretch of a river bank, for example, can be studied botanically, historically or geographically, according to the way in which one studies and the kind of conclusion one wishes to reach. It is in this latter that the essential differences between the disciplines lie; subjects differ in the kinds of thinking they are engaged upon. One then has to ask whether it is possible to integrate these kinds of thinking, as well as the various subject matters, or whether the differences are so fundamental as to make this impossible. It then appears that integration is possible in some spheres, but not in others. It would seem that botany and music, for example, could never be integrated, nor French with divinity, as both the subject matter and mode of thinking of these pairs are incompatible with each other. One is forced to conclude that our academic disciplines can never be completely integrated. The day will never come when we have one subject on the school timetable, called 'Knowledge'.

Inter-disciplinary studies, then, are unlikely to sweep away the old divisions in the schools altogether, for intellectual, economic and social reasons. Grouping is not suitable equally for all subjects, and for some, not at all. There is an important point here. When the significance of these differences between disciplines is not grasped, work of this kind can lead to a smattering of knowledge in many subjects, and a really deep knowledge of none. This would not matter so much were it not that the thought structure behind each subject does not become apparent until it has been explored in some depth, so that to deny a child this depth of knowledge is to impoverish him intellectually, perhaps permanently. On a practical level, the integrated approach to teaching can lead to difficulties of organisation. It often involves teachers working together, with perhaps large groups of children. Above all, there is a severe shortage of integrated textbooks. This is a great stumbling-block when it comes to putting theory into practice.

Against these dangers must be placed the great benefits that come from this sort of study. It is in harmony with the child's natural way of working and with important intellectual trends; it can give rise to a variety of stimulating activities; the individual teacher can gain greatly from being one of a team, breaking down the intellectual isolation that is sometimes a feature of the staff-room.

History is a subject that can be more easily integrated with others than most. Its subject matter is so vast that it can encompass any other discipline. Languages, science, geography, music, mathematics and even religious education can all be approached historically, and history has something to offer them all. The intellectual concept behind history, its time-perspective, is not exclusive of other thought disciplines. Having no special technique, its thought structure is so much less rigid than that of other subjects that history is easily adaptable.

For these reasons, integrated studies, when carried out in schools, nearly always include history. The essential point to remember about a study of this kind is that it must, involving as it does several bodies of knowledge, be given cohesion. This can be done in several ways. A study of this sort can be based on the child's interests, so that the child itself, as it asks questions and makes discoveries, leads the swing from subject to subject. Or an integrated study can be given cohesion by being dominated by one subject, so that, for example, the geographical features of an area are explained in terms of history, science and economics. One could turn this round and explain the history of an area in terms of science, economics and geography. Alternatively, the different subjects can be united by being grouped round a definite theme, like transport, earning a living, or perhaps a place. Local history more or less demands an integrated approach.

Let us take some definite examples. An environmental study could be based on a child's, or a class's interests. Starting with what they see around them, children could perhaps investigate the traffic that comes along the main road. This would involve them in graph-making, geography and elementary economics. They could then study a house, not necessarily a grand or famous one, and be led into history, and, if they studied the plants in the garden, into botany. They could watch the night sky and be introduced to astronomy. The possibilities are endless. Exciting as it is, this kind of approach makes heavy demands on the versatility of the teacher.

Sometimes inter-disciplinary work finds a spontaneous beginning in something that has captured the school's imagination. A party of children from a school I know recently visited France. This visit was such a success that when they got back these children were interested in everything French —history and geography as well as language. When I last heard of them, they were busily practising French songs and dances to perform for their hosts on their next visit. In this case, of course, the integrated study was given cohesion by its focal point being France and the French people.

The themes upon which integrated work can be based are endless. Apart from the conventional ones, there are those like animals, food and games, all of perennial interest to children. Suppose one undertook a study of the horse. The evolution of the horse could be studied, his biology, his economic role in different societies. Two contrasting roles would be seen in the feudal system and in the tribal society of the Red Indians.

What of the teacher's role when the class is organised for an integrated study? Firstly, it is apparent that it is the teacher, perhaps a team of teachers, who does the integrating. Nobody else can. This does not mean amassing a great deal of information to be passed on to the children. The aim of an integrated study should essentially be to introduce the children to a variety of different kinds of thinking, which is implicit in the subjects they explore. The teacher should bear this in mind when planning activities. It should further be borne in mind, particularly in view of the shortage of textbooks, that inter-disciplinary work needs more, not less, knowledge of one's own subject, simply because one has the added task of relating it to all the other fields of study. Often a group of specialist teachers will work together to produce a programme for the children. Team-work has its joys, but it can also have its horrors. Obviously, one should work with those with whom one wants to work. Forced integration, imposed from above, is never a success. The various responsibilities of the members of the team should be clearly defined and honourably carried out, otherwise either the strongest personality prevails over everybody else, or the whole project disintegrates.

The integrated study also faces the teacher with the practical task of organising the children. Not only may he himself well have to provide the material for them to work on, he may be faced with forty or more children all waiting to do different things. He will wish to give each as much personal attention as he can, but much of the time he must find a way of guiding individual children while not being physically present himself.

It is therefore at this point that I wish to discuss two skills that every teacher of history should develop. These skills are valuable whatever form of working organisation is adopted in the class-room. They concern the making of study-kits and the making of work-cards. The study-kit is a collection of material on which a child, or a group of children, can work, and in doing so, thoroughly explore a subject. This collection is enclosed either in a box or in a large folder. Several firms now produce study kits. The Macmillan series *Exploring History* has already been mentioned, and other kits include *Longman History Project Kits: Roman Britain, Saxons and Vikings, The Norman Realm, Tudor England, Mediaeval England*, and *Stuart Britain*. Then there are the *Storypacks*, published by Evans, which encourage children to work across the various subjects. Kits of this kind usually include pictures, diagrams, written explanations and suggestions of work for the child to do.

Work-cards act as guides through a subject. Each card consists of a sheet of questions to be answered and suggestions for further activities. Cards can be handed out to individual children, or groups of children, and can be used with any kind of material, such as books, pictures or even models. Their beauty is that they can be graded to suit children of varying ability.

Study-kits and work-cards are valuable ways of adjusting a complex situation to the needs of children. They are of great value in the unstreamed class, such as the history teacher usually meets, because they can be adjusted to individual needs. Both can be used in any kind of organisation within the class-room, and are particularly useful when the range of work is wide, as, for example, in an integrated study. Study-kits and work-cards represent the acceptance by the teacher of child-centred activity in the history lesson.

Valuable as the commerical products are, one can sometimes find them very strange to use. The pictures may seem garish, the written explanations do not quite make the points one would oneself make, the set-out seems complicated. In short, one is trying to adapt someone else's thinking to one's own children. Because this is difficult and the effect often unnatural, every teacher of history should be able to produce his or her own material. He may not possess the resources of the commercial firms, but he can build his material up over a period of time. The result will then be exactly tailored to his own teaching. Apart from this, he will have saved a considerable sum of money, for most of these kits cost between £3 and £4 each.

To take the study-kit first, this should possess certain characteristics. They are set out singly below.

The good study-kit should encompass a whole subject and yet divide up into several aspects, so that it can be used by the whole class, or groups of individuals.

The materials contained in it should be appropriate to the age and ability of the children who are going to use it.

It should employ as many varied approaches to the subject as possible. This means not confining itself to reading matter only but including things to see, such as pictures and film-strips, things to hear, such as records and tapes, and even things to touch. The inclusion of a variety of material not only makes the kit more interesting, it induces a deeper understanding of the subject. A child who has both read about a battle and seen a picture of it attains a better grasp of the issues than a child who has only done the reading.

The study-kit should be used actively. In fact it should be so designed that it *must* be used actively. This is vital, and it is where many study-kits fall down. In particular, what activity is incorporated often does not attract the child's interest. Activity is an essential part of the process of learning, so that one should spare no effort to imbue the material with this quality. It can be done in several ways, some of them quite ingenious. Here are a few random suggestions. Simple crosswords or games for the children to play can help them consolidate their knowledge. If one had built up a folder on 'Architecture', for example, and was trying to teach the children what characteristics were typical of the various periods, one could devise a historical 'Happy Families', so that the first player to collect seven examples of a particular style would win the round. Or one can require pictures or information, reproduced on variously shaped pieces of card, to be fitted into their appropriate spaces under large headings. Suppose the object was to distinguish between the Norman and Saxon armies of 1066. Pictures and descriptions of the Norman ships, knights and weapons would only fit into the spaces provided on a big sheet entitled 'Normans' and similarly for the Saxons. This exercise would be self-correcting, and this is obviously desirable whenever possible. Another suggestion would be to provide a cardboard picture-frame and ask for a picture to be painted and slipped into it. There are infinite possibilities depending on the compiler's ingenuity and what appeals to the children.

The last point involves the presentation of the study-kit. It should be orderly and attractive. Its presentation should reflect the habits of mind one is hoping to inculcate in the users, and a child should never be faced with a frightening mass of material. The fault with many folders is that the contents are not classified clearly enough. One can make full and imaginative use of different colours and shapes here, enclosing various aspects of the subject involved in differently coloured or shaped envelopes. Shoe-boxes make useful containers, and coloured envelopes can be made from sheets of sugar-paper stapled together, or even bright pieces of wallpaper. Labelling should be clear and simple.

For the purposes of illustration, let us suppose that we are building a study-kit for eight-year-olds on World War II. It can be contained in a shoe-box. Inside the box are four folders or smaller boxes, red, green, blue and yellow. The red box is entitled, 'Why war broke out'. Inside there is a map of Europe, a written explanation of the causes of World War II and a brief account of the main campaigns of the war. A work-card suggests that the map of Europe be traced or reproduced, and there is a crossword to be done concerning the outstanding personalities of the war and their contributions.

The green box is entitled, 'How the war was fought'. It contains pictures and diagrams of the fighting forces of the nations involved in the war, including ships, artillery and aircraft. There are large sheets of paper separately labelled, 'German Army', 'British Navy,' 'Italian Air Force', and so on, and the pictures of the fighting men and weapons have to be fitted into spaces provided. Also in the green box are boxes of Airfix soldiers, so that a pair of children or a group can stage and fight out a campaign for themselves. A battle scene is to be drawn and inserted in the card frame provided, or described in words. The suggestions are made on a work-card.

The blue box is labelled, 'The war on the Home Front'. Inside are written accounts—eye-witness accounts if they can be obtained—of air raids, rationing and what it was like to be in factory work during the war, or an evacuee. There is a recording of air raid sounds, including the siren, gun-fire and bombs bursting. (This is one of the sound effects records produced by B.B.C. Radio Enterprises (see page 153). Decca (see page 153) has a record of excerpts from some of the famous speeches of Winston Churchill.) Interesting objects can be included in the blue box, such as an old identity card, a ration book, a piece of shrapnel. A work-card asks the child to write an account of the war at home, using key words such as 'Spitfire', 'rationing', 'Winston Churchill'.

The yellow box is labelled, 'How the war changed the world'. It contains a map of Europe before the war, and another of its boundaries afterwards. This map is drawn on tracing paper and can be placed over the first one, so that the changes are clear. The child is asked to describe these changes in words. There are short written accounts of the rise of the United Nations, the rebuilding of Germany and Japan, and of the problems the war did not solve. These accounts are accompanied by pictures. Lastly, a book list for further reading is included. Some of the books are already on shelves in the class-room, so that, finally, the child is directed to the broader horizons of his own research.

Such a study-kit is not beyond the resources of most teachers. It would certainly be much cheaper, and, I think, much more fun than a commercially-produced kit, both for the teacher to make and the children to use.

The work-card also plays an important part in enabling the teacher to reach the individual child. It acts primarily as a guide through a subject. Like the study-kit, it should always be carefully adapted to the abilities of the boy or girl using it. The younger or less able the child, the simpler the wording should be, the larger the letters and the fewer the sentences. The work-card can be used in conjunction with the written word, a model, a picture, or even a sound record. The essential of the good card is that the suggestions set are made in such a way as not to limit the response of the child, but to widen its horizon. Many work-cards fail in this respect, and it should never be forgotten that the badly-constructed card can actually inhibit a child's thinking. For this reason, any questions asked, though clear in meaning, should encourage the boy or girl to say what he or she really thinks, and should not be so loaded that only one answer is possible. For example, a loaded question asked of the picture (reproduced on page 62) of a working-class street in Victorian England would be, 'Do you think it a pity that the people threw their rubbish into an open dustbin?' Only one answer is possible, and a not very fruitful one at that, 'Yes.' A better question would be, 'How do you think the people in the picture got rid of their rubbish?'

Like the study-kit, the work-card should encourage active learning, and should involve as many learning media as possible—the written word and pictures, as well as sound.

If we imagine a work-card constructed for us with the recording of air-raid sounds that was included in the study-kit on World War II, it might run as follows:

(1) What sounds can you hear in this record?
(2) What is happening? (The listener hears planes approaching after the siren; then heavy gun-fire, bombs exploding and finally advancing footsteps which abruptly cease.)
(3) When were air-raids on Britain at their worst? How did Britain combat them? (There should be books in the class-room from which this can be found out.)
(4) Paint an imaginary picture of an air-raid,
   OR, write a story about one,
   OR, find out how bombs and anti-aircraft guns were made.

This work-card aims at guiding the child through the material, finally to embark on his own research and use his own mind freely.

We have discussed at some length in this chapter the various ways there are of organising the class for the many varied approaches to the teaching of history that exist today. The different kinds of organisation may well overlap, or be used in conjunction with each other. The individual project can be used within the group; an integrated study may call for frequent explanations by the teacher to the whole class; a game may serve as an introduction to a project. It is true to say, however, that each method of organisation varies widely in its implications, both for the teacher and the class.

Far from belittling the role of the teacher, the re-thinking that has taken place concerning the meaning of education and the way in which children learn has greatly enhanced it. The teacher of history today must understand his own discipline thoroughly, and further, be able to relate it to other compartments of knowledge. He must be able to work with others, and to see his own subject as just one brilliant colour in the rainbow. He needs to understand the assumptions underlying the many approaches to the teaching of history that there are now, and to be able to apply these to the children he teaches. He needs new skills in order to do this.

In other more subtle ways the teacher's role has changed, or rather developed, and this not only in the matter of skills, but psychologically. According to the way in which he organises his class, his own relationship with it will differ. He remains the interpreter of the adult world, though it is a world far less harsh than it used to be, and one in which the line drawn between the child and adult is not so rigid. To this he must now add the role of being able to create an environment in which children can find themselves, sometimes working alone, sometimes with each other. In short, he must be able to enter the world of the child.

The history teacher has become a true educator.

7
Social Studies, Civics and the History Teacher

By social studies we mean the study of society; civics is the study of the individual's rights and duties in that society. These subjects are now often replaced or supplemented in schools, particularly among fifth- and sixth-formers, by current affairs, which concerns itself with the immediate events occurring in the world day by day.

The study of society has become increasingly popular in recent years for children of all ages, and in some schools it is replacing history. This, of course, is of great concern to those of us engaged in the teaching of history, both because it forces us to examine the validity of our own subject, and also, from a practical viewpoint, because it is usually the history teacher who is asked to take social studies. Certain questions need to be asked. What are the reasons behind the swing over to social studies? Should they replace history? Can the study of society offer anything history cannot?

The reasons behind the movement towards social studies and its allied disciplines are many: some are intellectual and some are of a practical nature. Of all the academic subjects, sociology and its sister subjects have the shortest history; they are really only as old as the twentieth century. The basic assumption of social studies is that we, in our society, form a community; that we, in Britain, have certain things in common and certain rights, duties and responsibilities towards each other. This may seem so obvious a truth to those of us who live in the twentieth century as hardly to need stating, but in fact, it was not always so.

It could be postulated that people in mediaeval times thought quite differently, feeling much more at one with others of the same social class in other countries than they did with those of a different social class in their own land. They may have felt, above all, that the one true community lay in the Church. In eighteenth-century England it seems clear that members of parliament saw themselves as representing their own localities and fighting for their interests against others if necessary—a far cry from the M.P. of today, whom we would see as, and who would himself claim to be, the representative of the interests of the whole of Britain. This conviction that we all form part of some community is therefore very recent. Several factors contributed to it. In England, a very strong cohesive force has been the law. Since Anglo-Saxon times the same law has bound us all, and each citizen has borne the burden of preserving the peace, irrespective of his rank. This is quite unlike France, where the divisions in the law helped to stratify French society. Another factor is the growth of a sense of nationality. There is disagreement among historians as to exactly when this can be dated in England, and even as to what it really is, as there always must be with so vague a concept, but many would place the emergence of this feeling in the fifteenth and sixteenth centuries, with the coming of the Tudors. This was when Englishmen clearly felt themselves to have more in common with one another than with, say, Germans or Spaniards. Also contributing to this sense of belonging to a community are factors of a much more recent origin, particularly those springing from the events following the Industrial Revolution in the latter half of the eighteenth century. Certain developments then welded parts of Britain physically into one, the most obvious being the development of transport and communications. After all, you cannot feel far apart from a person when you can step on to a train and see him in half an hour. He is much farther away if you have to walk the same distance of thirty miles in three days along rutted roads. Ease and frequency of meeting will probably also mean that you exchange ideas and customs and come to have more in common in a deeper sense as well. The growth of a national Press must similarly have contributed to a sense of unity. After all, today, many of us read the same newspapers.

A very important development was the growth in the power of the central government. This came about mainly because the Industrial Revolution caused problems so immense that they could only be dealt with by the power of the State. Factory conditions, poverty and unemployment all proved unamenable to any remedial action less than that which could be exerted by the central government. Throughout the nineteenth century the State extended its power over the lives of individuals until today we are all similarly bound by Acts of Parliament governing education, conditions of employment, housing and crime, whether we live in the Hebrides or in the heart of Liverpool. The growth of democracy, a movement that took place likewise in the nineteenth century, bound us all to one another in another sense, for now that we all have the vote we are, politically, equals. As is usually the case, these developments were quickly embodied in a political philosophy. Intellectuals such as the Fabians at the beginning of the twentieth century were quick to insist that the State has duties towards the welfare of its citizens, that we cannot close our eyes to the disease or distress of our neighbours, or they may soon be ours too. At the same time, new fields of knowledge and new techniques were being explored. Psychology, economics and anthropology came together to form a new discipline, sociology, or social science. These disciplines aimed to apply a scientific method to the study of society.

From the circumstances surrounding the evolution of this belief, that we are part of a community, spring the assumptions upon which the social disciplines are based. These assumptions are usually accepted as being obviously true and inevitable, but this is by no means the case. There is, for example, the insistence that the State has a duty to deal with social ills, but we would probably not believe this were it not for the far-reaching changes brought about by the Industrial Revolution and also for the decline in the belief in the religious nature of society. This latter means that the misfortunes of life, since they are now seen as man-made and not God-sent, and are no longer reckoned as contributing to our happiness in an after-life, should not be tolerated. There is also the assumption that all the members of our community bear a responsibility towards each other, and that society is an organism. This may be a useful piece of propaganda, and it has historical origins, but how far is it really true? It may well be that much of the strain of living in modern society stems from the fact that the individual is continually burdened with a sense of responsibility for the criminal, for the sick, for the aged, when there is little he can do about them. Responsibility without the power to act can lead to a disabling sense of guilt. So perhaps some of these assumptions need careful scrutiny.

It is clear, however, that the historical circumstances in which the study of society has grown up have dictated its characteristics as a subject. The community is seen as a collection of individuals who are equal in status, bound together by certain institutions, customs, rights and duties that they share in common. This community is studied scientifically, with the implication that what is not good shall be changed.

The practical arguments in favour of encouraging all schools to adopt social studies seem pressing. They are linked to the factors that made the development of social science as a subject inevitable in the first place. There is the simple fact that the network of rights and benefits possessed by the individual man or woman in the Welfare State has become so complex that many adults fail to understand it. We therefore have the ridiculous situation of the benevolent designs of the State being defeated by the sheer ignorance of its citizens, and those, usually, the ones most in need.

Then it seems to many people that one of the cornerstones of society, the acceptance on the part of its citizens that they have certain duties towards it, such as helping the police, voting in elections, and so on, is visibly crumbling. People no longer seem to care. There are also signs that the old moral values are disappearing. The answer on many peoples' lips is that 'it is up to the schools'. History cannot teach the children these lessons, but social studies and civics can and should.

At this point perhaps it is as well to examine the nature of history and social studies as subjects, and, in particular, to study their relationship to each other. One thing is already clear, and that is that the study of society is much better understood when it is put into its historical perspective. Only then do many of the assumptions that are often taken for granted reveal their relative, changeable nature. History, then, has much to offer social studies.

This is true in other ways. History and social studies have, at first sight, much in common, for they both study humanity. Both examine human institutions and experience. The essential difference between the two disciplines is that history works in a time-perspective and sociology does not. Sociology works in the present. Imagine a study of poverty undertaken by both a sociologist and a historian. The sociologist sets out to make a complete survey of poverty as it exists in our society at this moment in time, its causes, manifestations and perhaps its palliative. The historian sets out to make a study of poverty at some time in the past, and he is concerned continually with historical perspective. This gives him a standard of comparison between various phenomena that is in many ways more subtle than that which the sociologist possesses. The sociologist is able to compare, say, poverty as it exists today in English society with it as it exists contemporaneously in other societies. But phenomena that exist side by side in time are likely to be very similar to each other, or else to exist in a primitive society so different from our own as to make comparison difficult and not very profitable. The historian can compare poverty today with poverty as it existed in a society completely different from our own, because it existed so long ago. The contrast is usually profound. Twentieth century people tend to see all social problems in physical and material terms, to be given physical and material solutions. This is true of this intractable present-day problem of poverty whether it is seen in England or the Far East. The historian would be aware that the people of a mediaeval society would not see it in this light at all. Their way of alleviating physical distress would probably be to ease it by mental acceptance—a solution quite unacceptable to the twentieth-century mind. The long perspective in which the historian, of necessity, views his work can sometimes enable him to see a phenomenon more clearly, revealing more of its essential nature, than the sociologist can.

The historian has another advantage, in that he is concerned with evolution. To take an institution, for example Parliament, he will know how it has evolved from the time when it was, as its name implies, 'an opportunity for talking', to the mammoth of the twentieth century, embodying both the democratic ideal and the power of the modern state. He will form his own opinion as to what characteristics are essential in this institution, those that have survived the passage of time, and he may well have a shrewd idea as to how it might evolve in the future. In this way, the historian possesses a more subtle criteria of judgement than the sociologist.

History can also make us aware of the transience of social phenomena. This can be vitally important even in a practical sense. Often the members of a society will assume that their own institutions, their own ways of going about life, have an unalterable, absolute quality, when, in fact, they have not. Take a situation that is growing more and more urgent every day, the position of women in modern society. The problems that face them as they struggle to lead lives of their own as well as being wives and mothers seem much less intransigent when put in historical perspective. It is comforting to know that in days gone by there was no washing-up because everyone ate off bread and devoured it afterwards, and that there was precious little housework because ordinary families usually lived in one room. Women's problems are a product of our society, not of their intrinsic nature, and may pass away. The sociologist can make the same point in his own way, in that he can point to societies existing contemporaneously with our own where woman's role is different. However, the point can somehow be made much more vividly when the parallel is drawn from within one's own country, for it demonstrates that what is often assumed to be unchangeable can change.

The closeness of the sociologist's viewpoint to the phenomenon he is studying poses him with another problem. It is sometimes not easy for him to escape from his own moral viewpoint. Being so much a man of his age, he is apt insensibly to assume that his own attitudes are right; indeed, he may scarcely be aware of any other. Over such heart-searching issues that exist today (colour prejudice and class consciousness, for instance), the automatic assumption that most rational people living in the twentieth century would make is that these are totally wrong. Any investigation made of these issues would rest on this unspoken premise. However, to gain a real and complete understanding of these attitudes we need to be aware that in our society of the past they were not wrong. Translated into action, unawareness of this fact can lead to a dangerous assumption of moral rectitude, particularly on the part of the teacher. In the chapter on the organisation of the class the game 'Star-power' is described, which aims to change children's attitudes towards certain social problems, such as discrimination between people of different class and colour. It is quite possible that the teacher directing a game of this sort is, in fact, right regarding his attitude in our times and in our circumstances. However, he needs to be actually aware that he need not necessarily be, nor for all time. A knowledge of history can give him this awareness, which is surely the essence of true morality. History, then, has a great deal of valuable and pertinent comment to make about present-day social problems, by virtue of possessing the perspective that sociology lacks.

The two subjects also differ in their methodology. Sociology claims to apply the scientific method to social phenomena, though there is considerable dispute as to just how scientific this can really be. It does, however, aim to draw its conclusions from observed facts, and to apply the controlled experiment wherever possible.

If a sociologist were investigating, for example, the effect of the loss of the mother on children's behaviour, he would compare his observations of a group of such children with those of a group who had suffered no such loss. In this way, he would be able to estimate how far certain behaviour was typical of the deprived group. If it were also typical of the control group it would not be significant at all. Because of its strongly scientific nature, sociology relies heavily on statistics and the theory behind them. The historian, of necessity, is confined to a much less exact method of working. His raw material consists of written records and relics which were in the first place often themselves interpretations of the events and facts of the past. He cannot carry out a controlled experiment on the people of the past, or question them, because they no longer exist. Much of the information he would like is unavailable to him, either because it has been lost or because it never existed in the first place. His conclusions therefore must often involve an element of guesswork.

Nevertheless, the gap between history and sociology in this respect is less wide than it appears. The conclusions the social scientist draws from the statistics and information he collects must often possess a strongly subjective element, far more so than those of the natural scientist. This can be illustrated from two fairly recent surveys.

A short while ago statistics revealed that much more industrial injuries benefit was being paid out to the working population than had hitherto been the case. How were these figures to be interpreted? Could it be that the Acts of Parliament laying down safety conditions in factories were proving ineffective? Were workers growing careless? Neither of these solutions was the one offered. It was suggested that the working population had discovered that industrial injuries benefit was significantly higher than that paid out for sickness, and had acted accordingly. That this interpretation was correct could not, at the moment, be proved objectively; it depended in the last resort on a subjective judgement, based on a shrewd knowledge of human nature. Another matter that is causing grave concern at the moment is the incidence of violent crime. The statistics suggest that violent crime is increasing, a suggestion that is blazoned daily on television and in the newspapers. But is it? It is true that the figures for indictable offences are going up, but could this be partly because the police are more effcient, or because more crimes are reported? And might some of the causes lie, not in the permissive society, as is generally alleged, but in, say, the changing stresses on the institution of the family? For example, murder, the most violent crime of all, is most frequently carried out by a near-relative, usually a husband or wife on a marriage partner. Deciding on the interpretation of statistics is a highly complex matter, and not nearly so scientific as it appears to be. One of the dangers of the social services is that their conclusions may be accepted as objective and indisputable when they are not.

Another danger is that of equating the people behind the statistics with the statistics themselves. The social investigator is sometimes tempted to do this particularly because the statistical survey brings out what are uniform and stable characteristics in the population. Hence the cry of our time against 'the planners', who manipulate people's lives to fit in with a preconceived social plan. They do not take enough account of one of the essential characteristics of human beings—their unpredictability. Witness the world-record-breaking runner who yet never wins a race, or the child stricken by apparently incurable cancer who nevertheless wins the fight to live, or the diplomat kept a prisoner in one dark room for eight months, under constant threat of death, and who emerges sane and in perfect health. This unpredictability is rarely forgotten by the historian, for it is part of his stock-in-trade. His very lack of objectivity can make him, in a sense, more truthful.

The point of this discussion is that the study of history should be seen as inseparable from the study of society. History, by virtue of its time-perspective, can reveal what is enduring about society, and its structure. It can help us to be more truly objective and rational about our social problems, because it can reveal them as relative and transitory in a way that sociology cannot. Above all, it has a great deal of valuable comment to make about human nature, and this is what sociology is about. On the other hand, lest this be thought to be an attack on the social sciences, they too have much to offer. Many of the techniques of the sociologist have been adopted by the historian in recent years, to great effect. In the schools, the social sciences have a vital part to play in education. They can teach the individual to stand back from his own prejudices and to be as scientific as possible in assessing the society in which he lives. The individual child can come to a better understanding of what his own role in the community should be, of his rights and duties as well as of the work he may wish to do. The choice before the schools should not be between social studies and history, but on how to make them best go hand in hand.

Human beings are social animals, so that it goes without saying that the teaching of social studies should proceed harmoniously with the expanding relationships of the child. The key role of the teacher is to match his methods of teaching, together with the material he introduces, to the widening horizons of his class.

A young child becomes aware of his mother in the first instance, and then, after a few months, of his own family. In very early childhood his social awareness is bounded by the limits of his own home. By the time he is about two, though, his horizon has expanded to include what he deems to be the key figures in the world outside. Everyone will recognise these figures: they are those heroes of childhood such as the milkman, the dustman and the postman. These are the people who come to the child's own home. A little later he becomes interested in those who do not necessarily come into his own territory, but whom he sees on expeditions into the surrounding district. He may go shopping and make friends with the grocer and the fishmonger, or to the local park and get to know the old ladies and gentlemen sitting on the park bench. Most parents know to their cost that young children quickly understand what shops are for. Some of these people excite a tremendous interest among young children. This great interest seems to go beyond the bounds of mere friendship into what appears to be an early love-affair. I know a little boy who is desperately in love with the milkman and a little girl who cannot survive without visiting the dry-cleaner every single day. Intensely aware as a child may be of the key figures in his own environment, he does not yet relate them to each other, only to himself. While he is under five, he will be aware that the park-keeper and the coalman play an important part in his life, but not that they play a part in each other's.

While they are at this stage, the young boy or girl also become aware of certain procedures in our society and even of certain problems. These they re-enact in their games. The little girl of three who loves the dry-cleaner plays a game called 'Parking'. It consists of carefully manoeuvring her tricycle, scooter and trolley into line by the wall in her garden. She mutters anxiously 'Now, can I get out ?', 'No, I can't park here', 'I'll try over there!' and so on. She also plays 'Shopping', as many children do, though in the case of this little girl for some reason the shopkeepers never have any goods, and their only reply is, 'Don't keep it.' It is clear that, in their own way, children well under the age of five come to an awareness of society.

By the time they are five, children are beginning to perceive that there exists a certain social network. They realise that such people as the bus-driver and the lollipop lady have a connection with each other, as well as with themselves. It is at this point that what can be described as the teaching of social studies can begin, in the first years of school. The best approach is through the very people the children show such interest in. There are some excellent books on such people as the policeman and the fireman, in the Blackwell's *Learning Library* series. Some of the Ladybird books are of the same kind. Even more exciting is to meet some of these people in person, and to hear them talk about their work. They are often willing to come. Some of the children may well have fathers who are bus-drivers, or factory workers on shift work, who would enjoy a friendly visit to school. It is also the growing fashion for fire, ambulance and police stations to have 'open days', when the children can see round and inspect their equipment.

While they are still in this stage young children becomes very interested in the world of work. It is not just the personalities of the policeman and the fireman that excite them, but the exciting lives they lead. To introduce them to an understanding of society through the world's work is, therefore, a particularly apt approach. This kind of study need not necessarily centre on a person, but on a place, like a busy airport, a market or a railway station. In this way the children may come to appreciate something of the way in which society functions. They may realise, as they study the local market, for instance, why prices fluctuate, how the market is organised, the kind of lives the stall-holders live, with a different pattern of rising and going to bed from the rest of the population. Above all, they may understand the inter-dependence of most sections of society; to put it simply, how none of us can manage without the other. The stallholder could not sell his fruit unless the farmer grew it; it could not arrive at the central market unless it was brought there by train and lorry; once in the local market the Weights and Measures Inspector sees that we are not sold short weight. And none of these processes of production, buying and selling could take place without money. This kind of investigation lends itself to active integrated work outside the school; it can also be approached through either building up or working on a study kit. (The value of such work-kits and how the teacher can construct them is discussed in the chapter on the organisation of the class.)

Even when children are very young, they can, in their own way, grasp the existence of certain economic laws. When they see the laws of supply and demand governing prices in the shops, or when some of their fathers unfortunately become unemployed, these things should be noted and discussed in simple terms.

Children will understand the structure of society better, and possess a more critical standard of judgement, if they are led to put what they observe into historical perspective. Learning about the evolution of shops, transport and people's work all form part of social studies. Many books are now produced that are ideal for this purpose. To mention just a few, there are the *How and Why Wonder Books* by Transworld publishers, which are gay, coloured little volumes on a very wide variety of topics; there is the *History Workshop* series written by H.T. Sutton and G. Lewis and published by Cassells, which covers subjects such as the history of flight, the development of road and rail transport, and the achievements of space travel. Each book has a practical section, suggesting model-making for children of all ranges of ability. *Topics Through Time*, written by G. and J. Kent and published by the University of London Press, explores the world of work. Each volume tells the history of one trade or occupation, and include those of the housewife, the farmer, the inventor and the merchant. An exciting new venture has just appeared in the *It's Made Like This* books, published by John Baker. These explain how some of the inventions we take for granted, like cameras and films, actually work. The *How We Find Out* books published by the same firm explain how discoveries are made in fields like detection (surely very popular!), agriculture and food. There are also the *How To Run* books, which describe how service industries like airports and the railways are managed. Another interesting publishing venture is the *They Work with Danger* series, written by D. Smith and D. Newton and produced by Longman. These books describe the importance and hazards of certain occupations, specially picked because of the fascination they hold for young children. So far they cover the lives and work of the astronaut, the frogman, the game ranger and the steeplejack. All these books are suitable for young children.

Neither should one forget that social studies lend themselves to audio-visual aids. Sometimes charts such as those printed by the Pictorial Charts Educational Trust can provide a simple, clear analysis of a situation in visual form. These charts come with Teacher's Notes and include those on local government, the public purse and how the economy works. Some of the materially run industries, such as the Post Office, produce pictorial information about their work, specially for young children. *Treasure Chest for Teachers*, published by the Schoolmaster Publishing Company, is invaluable for providing other sources of material. Educational Productions Ltd also publishes charts for social studies, on local government and the law.

The adolescent presents rather a different picture from the younger child. On the other hand he is capable of much deeper and more critical analytical thinking, and is also more able to handle the abstract ways of thinking necessary for a penetrating investigation of society. On the other hand, he is concerned not merely with the way in which society works, but why it works, its end. These considerations are typical of the adolescent, but not of the younger child.

As we know these days to our cost, often the boy and girl approaching adulthood is dissatisfied with the way in which society is run, and decides to opt out. The adolescent, who is often the school-leaver, is again urgently preoccupied with his own immediate future. What matters most to him is to find out what is going to happen when he leaves school and enters the world of work. In the depths of his personality he has deeper worries. Often, under a disguise of lethargy or truculence, he is desperately concerned with his own personal relationships with the opposite sex, with his own family and with society at large. He knows totally different demands will soon be made on him, but he cannot quite see what these are, or whether he will be able to meet them. All these worries indicate the appeal that social studies should make to adolescent boys and girls. They should help them to a critical assessment on society, they should introduce them to the adult world and they should encourage them to think about their personal relationships.

In approaching social studies on a deeper level the teacher faces difficulties. For one thing, the history teacher (and it is usually he who, as a matter of course, is given the task of teaching social studies, on the ground that they are allied to history) has often little or no grounding in sociology. Another problem is that social studies, although talked about as though consisting of one discipline, consists in fact of many. It is a complex subject, involving a knowledge of economics, psychology, ethics, history and even anthropology. There are few easy textbooks for children. This is why teachers of social studies so often adopt either the study of an institution, like Parliament or local government, or the 'problem' approach, in an effort to give the subject some kind of structure. After all, social problems like housing or immigration have at least an intrinsic structure of their own. They all have causes, manifest themselves in certain ways and all, we hope, have solutions. Institutions also possess an inner coherence. It is, however, a pity to limit the teaching of social studies in this way, for it means that the picture the children will form of society will not be a true one. They will either think of it as a series of crises; or as a static arrangement of unchanging institutions, rather than the enduring but ever adaptable organism that it really is. They will lack perspective, being unable to relate the problem or the institution studied to the underlying social structure. All in all, it is much better for the prospective teacher of social studies to acquire an elementary grounding in the various disciplines involved first. If he intends, for example, to carry out any kind of social survey he will need an elementary knowledge of statistics; he will need to know something of the significance of the random sample and how to conduct a simple controlled experiment.

There are several good books published by Penguin on general economics and sociology. *The Economics of Everyday Life*, by Gertrude Williams, is a well written, intensely readable book, and a good one to begin with. Another excellent Pelican is *Statistics for the Teacher*, by A. C. Crocker. This, as its title suggests, explains the concepts underlying statistics and indicates ways in which the teacher can apply them to work in the class-room. The Butterworth Group of publishers produce rather more advanced books on various aspects of sociology and economics. One that would be very useful is the *Dictionary of Economic Terms* edited by A. Gilpin.

Recently the Schools Council has completed a research project on the teaching of social studies in primary and secondary schools. The research team was led by Dr Denis Lawton and has produced a report containing many suggestions as to how this teaching can be developed. It is the Schools Council *Working Paper 39: Social Studies 8–13*, and is published by Evans/Methuen Educational. Following the recommendations of the research team, the Schools Council has set up a curriculum development project in order to produce teaching materials. This sounds very hopeful for teachers of social studies.

Having grasped the essentials of the subject, the teacher can lead his class in a series of field investigations. An interesting analysis would be that of the national and local Press. This can be done in terms of space initially, by measuring with a ruler the size of headline and the amount of space given to such topics as crime, political discussion, fashion, strip cartoons and so on, in a selection of newspapers. Then an attempt can be made to assess the slant of newspapers and how far an item of news is consistently reported day by day. Occasionally one can try to assess the veracity of a newspaper's reporting. In this way, a picture of the Press can be built up, its aims and methods of communications. Other kinds of survey that older children can carry out would be an analysis of the local traffic, or the organising of opinion polls on controversial issues.

The social survey goes some way towards giving an objective picture of some of the institutions, customs and opinions we treasure in our society. As it is sometimes criticised because it apparently equates people with statistics, it is as well to consider ways of preserving the human element. One colourful way of doing this is to use a portable tape recorder. Then the views of various people can be collected to add meaning to the statistics, and later played to the rest of the class. The children themselves can easily do this, provided always, of course, that if they are interviewing strangers they go in pairs or small groups. There are many enlightening and amusing occasions when statistical conclusions can be illumined by people's personal views on the subject. I remember one occasion when a pair of teenagers had gone round collecting the views of a variety of people on capital punishment. They had tried to get a cross-section of views from all social classes in order to see if there were any persistent trends. One of the people interviewed was the local barber. To the polite question, 'Have you any views on capital punishment, sir?' there came a long, heavily breathing pause and then, 'Nah!' This barber was one of the 'don't knows' of the public opinion polls, but his comment probably did more than any other to add depth to the investigation.

Field investigations, usually in the locality, can be given meaning in human terms in another way. They can be combined with active social service on the part of the children. This kind of work is very popular in schools today, and the forms it takes are many. Older boys and girls redecorate the homes of old people or dig their gardens, younger ones run errands, grow flowers for the blind, prepare a concert for the local home for the disabled—the possibilities are endless. There are many benefits to this kind of work, some of them not at first obvious. First and foremost, it is a great thing simply to be able to help someone else in need, and children, who, after all, are the weakest and most immature members of society, deeply appreciate this. It wins them approval and they gain in self-confidence. It also makes them identify with the problems of other people less fortunate than themselves, and to accept that in any real community it is the role of the strong to help the weak. Intellectually, the experience they gain adds a new and somewhat rare dimension to the scientific approach they adopt towards social phenomena in the class-room. It is one thing to reflect upon the statistics concerning the aged in our population while sitting comfortably in school, quite another to visit an old lady every Saturday afternoon who is invariably bad tempered, rude and ungrateful, and who always begs you, with tears in her eyes, to come again. The human experience illuminates the social problem.

Active social work can also help regarding another problem commonly met in the teaching of social studies. This is the problem of 'double-think'. It is not uncommon to find children adopting one attitude in the class-room and reserving quite another for 'real life' outside school. They are quite capable of writing convincingly as to why colour prejudice is wrong in their social studies lesson, and then ganging up on a group of West Indians on the way home. Adults are even more clever at 'double think' than children are. The problem is a fundamental one, with a bearing on the very nature of education, and the relevance of school life to that outside. It can be partly countered by giving children as much contact as possible with the world outside school, for when one actually has to live out one's thoughts as one does when one is acting on them, they soon become tailored to what one truly believes.

This special survey together with work in the locality then has an important part to play in social studies. Two things need to be remembered. If the studies are local in nature, and they are likely to be, they need to be given both a wider perspective, by relating them to nation-wide issues, and a deeper perspective, by showing the evolution in time of the trends investigated. After all, poverty in rural Scotland may not be at all the same kind of problem as poverty in a London suburb, and it will be useful to know what has happened in the past. A wider perspective can be gained by reading. Her Majesty's Stationery Office publishes a great number of reports, statistics and the findings 'of inquiries, many of which have a nation-wide significance. Particularly useful in gaining this wider view are the charts produced by companies such as the Pictorial Charts Educational Trust (see page 154), and which present a synopsis of a subject as it reveals itself over the whole of Britain. There are, for example, charts on colour prejudice, one on Britain's Health Service, and another on advertising.

A great deal can be revealed about an institution, custom or problem if it is put into its historical perspective, and there are now many interesting books which do this. The following, some of which use the documentary approach, are particularly appropriate for the adolescent and school leaver. There is the series by K. Dawson and P. Walls) *Society and Industry in the Nineteenth Century* (Oxford University Press), which explains the evolution of parliamentary representation, factory reform, the trades unions, poverty, and housing. The *Exploring History* series (Macmillan) consists of teaching kits constructed for the average child, and deals with subjects such as Transport and the Industrial Revolution. Assignment cards come with these kits. Penguin produce the *Topics in History* series, which gives accounts, through original documents, of public health from 1830 to the present day, of the development of the Welfare State, and of Westerners in the Far East.

As has already been mentioned, H. T. Sutton and G. Lewis have devised a *History Workshop* (Cassell) in twelve books, covering transport, voyages of adventure, life in earliest times and in the days of the Romans, the Tudor era, and so on; the final topics are *Into Modern Times* and *Into the Space Age*. These are written for primary pupils, but are quite suitable for the older child. Cyril Niven has written some useful books showing how many of our ways of doing things have evolved through time. These are the *Journey Through the Ages* books (Holmes McDougall) and describe the evolution of modes of communication, science and medicine. The *Today is History* series (Blond Educational) speaks for itself. It aims at showing the relevance of the past to the present day, and numbers among its fourteen titles the history of trades unionism and of protest.

Other books with a more general slant are those that cover present social, constitutional and international history. Examples are the *Journey Through History* books, written by S. E. Gunn (Edward Arnold) and the series *Britain Past and Present* by M. W. Thomas (Nelson). The latter includes books on the working people of Britain and on daily life.

There also exist some excellent audio-visual materials. The Longman *Modern Times* L. P. records offer comments by distinguished men and women on subjects very relevant to social studies, such as the making of the Welfare State. So does Sussex Tapes (Educational Productions Ltd of Wakefield). Then there are television and sound broadcasts, by both the B.B.C. and the independent organisations. The B.B.C., for example, has offered a continuing series of television programmes for pupils of 14–16 on British social history in the nineteenth and twentieth centuries, and so has I.T.V. The use of such sources in the classroom is discussed in the chapter on audio-visual aids.

Speakers on special aspects of society are greatly appreciated by the older boy and girl, bringing as they do a breath of air from the world they will soon make their own. The local Council may have its own Public Relations Officer. I remember an occasion, in one of the schools in which I taught, when the Mayor himself came, resplendent in chain of office. The first question he was asked by an eager fourth former was why she still had to pay a penny to use the public lavatory outside the Town Hall. Many societies have speakers willing to speak about specific problems such as drugs, housing and the aged. All this helps to give the social survey the depth, humanity and even the mental honesty it needs.

An approach to the teaching of social studies that has a particular relevance to the older boy and girl is through the world of work that he or she is about to enter. This should go hand in hand with a consideration of the mature personal relationships of adult life. The individual child is certainly pre-occupied with the work he may choose or be forced to do when he leaves school, but underlying this is his anxiety about the whole network of human relationships that bind together the adult community, in work, in the family and at leisure. The concept of responsibility, for example, is concerned in all these. What is the school leaver's responsibility to his employer, his girl-friend, his parents, himself? And what is their responsibility towards him? His concern goes much deeper than merely getting a job, and here social studies and ethics really go hand in hand. The school-leaver needs help in another respect; this is in the sheer mechanics of being a citizen in a compli-cated society. He needs to know about sickness and unemployment benefit, how to get on the housing list, even how to write a cheque and answer the telephone. It would not be too far-fetched to claim that lessons in make-up for girls and grooming for boys should be part of social studies.

An investigation of the working world is popular in schools. Some go-ahead schools devise schemes in which the children, though technically still with them, go to work in factories and offices and so gain first-hand experience. A difficulty is that this can meet with objections from the trades unions. The Schools Council Humanities Curriculum Project is an interesting attempt to provide, as nearly as possible, first-hand experience of the outside and working world for children without them actually leaving the class-room. The project as a whole aims at helping young people to understand complex social and moral issues, using a study-pack approach. It consists of 8 separate packs (all published by Heinemann) on *Education, War and Society, The Family, Relations between the Sexes, Poverty, People and Work, Law and Order,* and *Living in Cities.* Packs include tape-recorded interviews, photographs, games to play, and a teachers' handbook.

The Schools Council has also launched (1971) a project on Careers Education and Guidance, and materials for teachers and pupils are currently (1972–3) undergoing trials. (Later, they are likely to be published.) The project interprets careers education in a wide sense: while it includes knowledge of the basic facts about employment, it must also concentrate on helping young people to understand fully the world of work, to form a realistic assessment of themselves, to acquire the necessary skills for decision making, and to develop sufficient social competence to cope with the varied situations in which young adults find themselves when they enter employment.

These two schemes aim at employing as direct an approach as possible. Short of actually doing a job oneself, there is probably nothing quite so informative as hearing about it from someone who does it every day. One should therefore leave no stone unturned in an effort to find interesting speakers for one's children. They can be representatives of industry, or they can be the friends and relatives of children in the class, or they can be boys and girls who have recently left school. These last, in particular, can teach us a lot about the problems of boys and girls when they first go out to work. I remember one girl of sixteen who returned to talk of her experiences. She was sad and disillusioned, and told the others that the greatest shock had been when nobody rose when she entered the room. She was a lowly office-girl, and her ideas of what to expect had obviously been gleaned from cheap paperbacks. A boy of similar age was appalled by the swearing and pilfering of his older workmates, who, he had been led to believe, were to guide him in his new life. The opportunity to talk with others of one's own generation who are already in the working world can do much to avoid such anguish.

The B.B.C. produces some very good programmes to help school-leavers. Recently there has been a radio series, *The World of Work*, planned, in the words of the producers, 'to give help, information and self-confidence to school-leavers as they choose their careers and settle down to work'. The television programmes *Going to Work* (for less academic pupils) and *A Job worth Doing ?* (for those leaving after O-levels or their equivalent) are also designed to help with a choice of career. Also on television, under the general title *Scene*, there has been a series of short plays specially written for the less academic fourth and fifth former, presenting such issues as 'being away from home', 'finding a job to suit you', and 'attitudes to young marriage'. *Inquiry* is a radio programme with similar aims.

Several publishers have responded to the needs of the school-leaver by producing books about working life. Some of those already mentioned as appropriate for younger children are also suitable for the older boys and girls, such as the *They Work with Danger* books (Longman). Others have been written specially for the older child. Examples are those under the general title *Serving our Society* (Allman): subjects include *Men and the Boats*, *The Fire Service*, *The Police*, *Men against Disease*, *The Weathermen*, *The Town Councillor*, and *The Farmer*.

In the last few years there has been an imaginative attempt to introduce the school leaver to working life somewhat differently. The result has been a new and interesting range of books, which try to explain the world not merely in objective terms, but from the point of view of the teenager who is entering it. They deal with such moral perplexities as the drug scene, the pop world, as well as the more conventional issues such as pollution and the problems of peace. One venture of this sort is *Connexions*, published by Penguin. The series includes such titles as *Foreign Places, Foreign Faces*, which examines the reasons why people leave their own countries and what they find when they do; *Out of Your Mind?*, a focus on drugs; *Violence*; *Work*; and *For Better, for Worse*, an appraisal of marriage and the family. This is a real attempt to look behind the conventions of working life in our society, to the realities of choice and responsibility which govern everyone's conduct. The authors have tried hard to present these issues in a form palatable to teenagers, using pop songs, poetry and photographs to illustrate their themes.

Other publications aim at putting the issues before children in a more abstract, but none the less penetrating way. To mention just a few, there is M.V.C. Jeffrey's *You and Other People* (Ginn), written expressly to encourage the fifteen- to seventeen-year-old into discussion. There are chapters on 'Being Yourself', 'Doing One's Own Thinking' and 'Values'. Two books by K. Lambert, under the general title *Life in our Society* (Nelson), examine the problems of the individual boy or girl, at home, at work and in the larger community. Seen in this way sociality and morality become interchangeable terms, for our moral standards must of necessity be applied to our working lives. By skilfully introducing the older boy and girl to the life that awaits them outside school one can ensure not only that they are in a position to choose the best opportunities for themselves, but that they understand something of the place of work in our society and can integrate it with their own lives.

The teenager has yet another urgent need. He needs to be provided with information on the sheer mechanics of living in a society of bewildering complexity. It only needs one moment's thought to appreciate just what puzzling decisions await the average breadwinner as he enters upon his adult role. He may need to open a bank or Giro account, to work out what portion of his wage he should allot to living expenses, leisure and saving; he needs to understand Income Tax and to understand what is implied in hire purchase; when he gets married he will want to know how to get on the local authority's housing list; if he is ever out of work he will need to know what sickness and unemployment benefits he is entitled to, and how to claim them. Girls have exactly the same problems, together with the added ones of needing to know something about child care and the facilities the local clinic offers; one could add family planning. It is a sad fact that many people do not claim the benefits they are entitled to, simply because they do not know how to, and these are usually the people most in need.

In my opinion these things should be simply taught. All the appropriate forms can be obtained from the various government departments and they can be gone through together. Often it is possible to arrange talks from people such as the local Bank manager on how to open an account, or from the Health Visitor on how the clinic can help. A growing number of books are being written in order to prepare the school leaver in this way. There are, for example, the six *Topical Research Work Books*, published by Longman. Specially written for the average school leaver, they provide information in a lively way on such matters as designing a home, food to eat, having a job, and similar matters. They are sold only as a set. The *In Focus* books (Nelson) include one on *Managing your Money* by M. W. Thomas, which is a straightforward guide to wage deductions. Another, *Looking after Yourself* by Joanna Lockett, deals with the problems of girls living away from home for the first time—sharing a flat, going for an interview, looking after one's appearance. Some firms, incidentally, provide excellent free speakers for schools. Boots the Chemists will provide demonstrated lectures on make-up.

It would not be beyond the ingenuity of most teachers to construct work-kits on subjects like these, or to build one up with the children. In this way the children would have the material actually before them. How to set about this is described in the chapter on the organisation of the class. One or two commercially produced kits do, in fact, exist, such as the one on Money Management produced by Educational Productions Ltd. (see page 154).

If the teacher of social studies is to do his or her work well in the grounding of their children with regard to their social rights, it is essential that the teaching should be as realistic as possible, in the sense that somehow the division between school and the world outside should be broken down. Recently, a group of investigators found that most of us gain a far better idea of our social rights through watching the popular television serials like *Coronation Street* and *Cross-roads*, than we do from all the informative leaflets that are poked through our letter-boxes. The radio serial *The Archers* proved equally helpful. It is, perhaps, significant that *The Archers* was devised by the B.B.C. general service more than twenty years ago in order to educate people about farmers and the countryside. It tends to suggest that the somewhat dull matters of social benefits and legal rights may be best understood when approached in a relaxed atmosphere. Many people, and this includes children, are frightened of anything that smacks of 'them', or the government. A dramatic presentation may be valuable, making the information more digestible. It might be an idea, for instance, to present the class with situations in a dramatised form and ask them to find solutions from among the leaflets, information and even study-kits provided. Or they could dramatise their own situations and present them to each other. Failing all else, one could settle down and watch *Coronation Street* oneself in the evening, and base one's teaching on that!

There are, then, a variety of ways of teaching social studies to older boys and girls, bearing in mind their urgent needs to reflect upon society, to investigate it and to equip themselves for living in it.

Civics and current affairs are allied to social studies, in that they are both concerned with a study of society. However, they have much narrower boundaries. Civics is concerned with the learning of one's rights and duties as a citizen. This is considered more and more important these days, because there seem to be signs that many young people are opting out of both. In fact, when I mentioned this to a group of students recently I was told that the assumption on which civics teaching is based is quite immoral, and that it was really a form of propaganda on the part of the Establishment. This view deserves careful consideration; certainly the moral premises on which such teaching is based call for discussion in the class-room. But granted this, it is at least useful in the practical sense for everyone to know their voting rights, or that they are required by law to fill in their Census forms, and that they have certain rights if they are arrested by the police.

Many books are written nowadays for the purpose of explaining citizenship to children. *The People's Government* by K. Gibberd (Dent) and its companion volume, *Citizenship through the Newspaper*, have always been popular. Nelson has produced a series in three books, called *Citizenship for School Leavers*, by M. W. Thomas. Book 1 deals with the family and the social services; Book 2 covers local affairs; and Book 3 is concerned with affairs at national level. A book in greater detail is Jack Harvey's *How Britain is Governed* (Macmillan). Such books are not difficult to find. Reading can be supplemented by the various charts on civics which are published by the companies mentioned earlier in this chapter.

Recently, quite a new way of arousing children's interest has been thought of by Dr Eric Midwinter, the Project Director for Liverpool's Educational Priority Area Project. He has devised a game for them to play, called 'Streets Ahead'. The purpose of this game, in the words of the teacher's notes, is 'to strengthen children's awareness of their city environment, by simulating, through the "game" medium, city problems and situations'. In playing one round of the game, each child comes to understand four aspects of city life. There is scope for individuality as players adopt names of streets of their own choosing, and the teacher can modify the game to suit his class's special needs. Details of the game, or the game itself, can be obtained from Priority, of Liverpool (the address is given on page 152). It seems to hold infinite possibilities.

In the opinion of many luckless history teachers, who are usually given the task, current affairs is far more difficult to teach than either social studies or

13 GETTING HELP

1 When would a family seek help from

a district nurse? _____

a home help? _____

a health visitor? _____

Ministry of Social Security? _____

the W.V.S.? _____

a magistrate? _____

2 Mention two ways in which a policewoman can help members of a family.

   a _____   b _____

3 Write down two ways in which a family can get help in case of need for children attending school.

   a _____   b _____

4 What help could the family have for

a child recovering from a long illness?   a child remaining an extra year at school?

_____   _____

a child suffering from a nervous breakdown?

_____

5 Mention two ways in which a Probation Officer can help a family in case of need.

   a _____   b _____

6 What help can you get to continue your education after you leave school?

   a _____   ·b _____

7 In what ways can older members of the family be helped by the local council?

   a _____   b _____

GROUP WORK

1 On a map of the neighbourhood mark the places from which you could get speedy help (a) from the police, (b) from the fire service, (c) from the ambulance service.

2 How do you think help could be given to mothers who are not able to go out to work because they have young children?

3 What could local councils do to help (a) old people, (b) lonely people?

28

A typical page from the series Citizenship for School Leavers, Book I—The Family, *by M. W. Thomas (Nelson) (actual size $9\frac{3}{4}'' \times 7\frac{3}{4}''$)*

civics. This is mainly because it lacks a structure of its own as a subject; one simply flits from world crisis to crisis, usually in one lesson a week. Because the time allotted is so little, the teacher is faced with the seemingly impossible task of relating the main events of the week to the deeper world trends that have brought them about. Current affairs is usually an 'extra', never an examinable subject, so that there is often a marked reluctance on the part of the class to do any background reading. For these reasons the whole burden seems to fall on the teacher, who often feels, as one of my colleagues described herself, 'like a performing flea'.

One can draw some comfort from the fact that various people are now paying more attention to the needs of teachers who take current affairs. These needs are, surely, to be able to present to one's class succinctly and attractively the issues of the day, and at the same time to be able to relate them to the more fundamental trends in world history. The following publications go a long way to meet such needs. Some of them, appropriately, are services provided by newspapers. *The Times* publishes *Issues of Today*, which consist of accounts of problems in the news, together with their historical background. For example, the issue *Race in Britain* gives the history of recent immigration and the facts about the numbers of immigrants, together with an outline of recent legislation. It may be obtained from *The Times* Special Publications (see page 153). Other titles in the same series are *Industrial Relations*, *Inflation*, *The Common Market*, and *Communist Powers*. Then there are *The Observer* News Bulletins for schools. These are special reports from overseas correspondents, sent red-hot from the scene of action, and are obtainable on subscription. *The Times* Special Publications also publishes *Topics*, a venture aimed at provoking discussion on current affairs. Each folder contains up to one hundred clippings from newspapers; so far three subjects are available, on *Television*, *Charity*, and *Censorship*, and each costs £1.00 (1973).

The *Sunday Times* (see page 153) provides a regular current affairs film-strip service for schools on subscription (currently £10 a year, 1973). Film-strips and teachers' manuals are sent three times a term, on such world-wide and interesting issues as *Sport as Big Business*, *Transplantation Surgery*, *The Making of the American President*, and more recent titles include *The Crisis of the Cities: Development or Decay?* and *Censorship: A Licence for Freedom?*

One or two organisations send out regular reviews of current affairs. For example, the Atlantic Information Centre for Teachers (see page 153) which publishes an international review called *The World and the School* three times a year, also sends out to its subscribers *Crisis Papers* which are produced quickly in response to current events.

Focus is a class-room newspaper in wall-chart form, which aims at capturing the interest of children in the nine to thirteen age range. It presents current issues clearly and simply in pictorial form and is produced fortnightly by E.S.L. Bristol (see page 154).

Quite clearly, the study of current affairs cannot be divorced from the study

The VAT man cometh

Bicycles, cameras, sweets, chocolates, record players and other goods are cheaper today than they were last week as a result of Britain's new taxation system – Value Added Tax (VAT) – which came into force yesterday. Other goods such as furniture, carpets and adults' clothes are now dearer.

Like Purchase Tax and Selective Employment Tax which it replaces, VAT is basically a tax on spending. Under VAT, ten per cent of the price of everything you buy (except for a few VAT-free goods such as food) is paid to the Government. Unlike the old taxes, however, VAT is not paid in one lump sum but is collected at every stage in the production of goods or services (see panel).

Britain has adopted VAT primarily in order to conform with other Common Market countries, which each operate a similar taxation system. But supporters of VAT say that the new tax has many independent advantages. Because it is collected at several stages, VAT is hard to evade. VAT is also 'fairer' than Purchase Tax because one tax rate (ten per cent at present) is spread over a wide range of goods. Under Purchase Tax there were three tax rates and the bulk of the revenue came from 'luxury' goods which bore the highest tax.

Opponents of VAT say that taxing essential and luxury goods at the same rate is *not* fair: it helps the rich at the expense of the poor. Moreover, VAT will increase the cost of living. Although prices in general are expected to rise by only one per cent as a direct result of VAT, some shop-keepers may make unnecessary increases which will be hard to detect during the change-over period.

The most widespread criticism of VAT is that it is very bureaucratic. It has been estimated that the paperwork of British firms will increase by 15 per cent and that 6,000 additional civil servants will be necessary to process the new tax.

HOW VAT WORKS

Lady Well-To-Do sells wood from her forest to Mr. Chips the toymaker. The wood for one toy train costs 50p plus ten per cent tax (5p) paid to the tax man.

Mr. Chips buys the wood for 50p plus 5p tax and makes a train. He sells the train for £1 plus 10p tax. But since 5p tax has already been paid, he sends only 5p to the tax man.

Mr. Gruff the shopkeeper (above) pays Mr. Chips £1 plus 10p tax for the train. Mr. Gruff sells it for £1.50 plus 15p tax. But since 10p tax has already been paid, he sends only 5p to the tax man.

Freddy Smith has now bought the train for £1.65. The untaxed train cost £1.50 but Freddy has also (indirectly) paid 15p to the tax man.

THE OLD AND THE NEW

Old taxes	New taxes
	Special tax on cars £125 m
SET £200 m	
Purchase tax £1,275 m	Value added tax £1,475 m
Total £1,475 m	Total £1,600 m

Focus 39, *2 April 1973—a part of the wall newspaper for the fortnight issued by ESL Bristol (actual size of the complete wall-chart is 36" × 47")* of world history. What hits the daily newspaper headlines is always related to trends in the world at large. International history is, in a sense, an extension of social studies. Many of the forces which moulded our society into one are now at work in the international field too, forging that also into one community. It is now possible to travel the length of the world in a matter of days, bringing diseases from which this country had long since thought itself immune back into our society. We cannot, therefore, any longer disregard the famine and malnutrition that exist in areas many thousands of miles from our own for, in a really frightening sense, the problems of those areas are ours too. Ease of communication has also its advantages, for it brings the peoples of the world much closer together in thinking and customs, making what once appeared freakish and outlandish now familiar. In economic terms, it is now quite clear that the fate of one country intimately affects another. One can instance the dependence of Britain's prosperity on the supply of materials from abroad, the increased cost of which has pushed domestic prices far beyond our wildest speculation, and made nonsense of governmental promises. Older people can remember the bitter price Great Britain paid for the American recession of the 'thirties. It is becoming increasingly apparent that national problems can only be solved by a study of international conditions.

In a more positive sense, there is a growing feeling that we share with other peoples of the world a common humanity. People today are frequently accused of being immoral, but in the concern they show for the sufferings of people far away they demonstrate a much more sensitive morality than was possessed, say, in the nineteenth century. Possibly the sciences have helped in this, in demonstrating so convincingly the common physical heritage of the human races. As religious barriers break down, too, the spiritual divisions that have hitherto divided people from people tend to fade away, so that, in a sense, the decline of the Churches means a more deeply-felt sense of community. For all these reasons, it is slowly becoming accepted that to be a citizen of one's own country means to be a citizen of the world.

International history is becoming popular in schools; like the study of our own society, it implies an understanding of the world's problems in the present day and age, and also a knowledge of the world's history. The teaching of it has one or two drawbacks, in that it tends to become both impersonal and materialistic. These tendencies spring from the nature of the subject. World history often seems impersonal because the forces at work in the world are so vast that they seem only capable of expression in abstract terms; it often appears materialistic because, again arising from the vastness of the subject, it is usually taught in terms of world problems and these are seen as largely physical. To teach it in this way not only makes it unappealing and difficult to understand, it also omits what is most precious. The history of the other peoples of the world should surely include an appreciation of their culture and of the great contributions that the civilisations have made to each other. At the moment it is quite possible for children to know quite a lot about famine and disease in present-day India, and yet be ignorant of the fact that the Indian civilisation was one of the oldest in the world. They may have heard of the politics of the Suez Canal, and yet not know that the Ancient Egyptians, thousands of years ago, were one of the earliest peoples to write and record a literature, many of whose stories make very good reading today. Here again, this can be put right by a knowledge of history. There is also need for really imaginative teaching, for it is no easy task to come to understand the culture of a community quite different from one's own.

There are two ways, little used at present, of leading children to an almost intuitive understanding of other peoples, and that is through their literature and their music. All children love a story, and some of the best and most beautiful stories come from other lands. Some of these are mentioned in the chapter on the approach, the story and the book. Many books of American, Russian, Chinese, African and other stories can be obtained quite easily from the local public library. It is a difficult exercise to draw abstract lessons about the various civilisations from these writings, and I think, quite an un-necessary one. By allowing children simply to enjoy them, as they would the stories written in their own language, one is encouraging them to appreciate a foreign culture on equal terms with their own.

Just as literature speaks to our common humanity, so does music. Musi-cians, with justice, are apt to object when they hear music described in verbal terms, but it is surely true that the music of people of other lands reflect themselves and their lives. This applies both to classical music and to folk song. Topic Records (see page 153), a firm which produces recorded folk songs especially as an aid to teaching in schools, has already been mentioned in the chapter on audio-visual aids. If some of the titles of these songs are quoted, their relevance to international studies will be seen. There are, for example, the infectious Yugoslav dances, and 'Come along, John' which is a collection of American children's songs on the same lines as our own 'Ring-a-Ring-a-Roses'. Younger children would enjoy these particularly as they are action songs. Then there are the songs and dances of Argentina, Australia and America, telling of the sufferings as well as the joys that the people lived through in their history. One should not overlook the resources of one's own class. West Indian and Indian children love to sing the songs and perform the dances of their own peoples.

Yet another way of helping children towards a real, sympathetic feeling for other peoples is to bring men and women from foreign countries into the class-room. Personal contact of this kind always conveys the feel of another culture much more subtly than an informative account from the teacher. Those of us who live in cities and rub shoulders with people of other natio-nalities know that it is the little things about them, the way the West Indians dress in brilliant colours, the music they like, the way they shop, that speak to us of customs quite different from our own. Various organisations are wil-ling to send speakers to schools, among them the Council for Education in

World Citizenship, which also organises youth conferences on world affairs. The addresses of this and similar organisations can be found in *Treasure Chest for Teachers*.

If one knows one's class, all sorts of other ways will occur of teaching them about foreign lands. Many children, for example, are avid collectors of stamps, and every stamp is really a little mine of information about its country of origin. There are many exciting ways of approaching the subject.

In the more conventional teaching of world affairs, there is now an increasing number of good books to help the history teacher. Particularly interesting and full of ideas are the curricula with a world approach which can be obtained from Oxfam (for address, see page 153). These curricula range from those suitable for young children to those suitable for older boys and girls, and they have actually been tried out in schools. They are full of interesting suggestions, such as introducing young children to the lives and problems of other peoples by showing them, first, a typical meal from each country. Oxfam also provides films and charts on world problems, often just for the price of postage.

As has already been mentioned, three times a year the Atlantic Information Centre (see page 153) publishes a review called *The World and the School*, especially for teachers.

J. L. Henderson has written a very useful book, *Education for World Understanding* (Pergamon), which is full of ideas for teachers of children of all ages. Another helpful book is *History Syllabuses and a World Perspective*, edited by A. Lyall and published by Longman jointly with the Parliamentary Group for World Government. This Group, one of whose aims is to promote world understanding, also produces pamphlets. *World Studies Bulletin*, largely prepared by the Group, is published four times a year as a supplement to the journal *New Era* (the journal of the World Education Fellowship). A full list of its publications can be obtained from the Parliamentary Group for World Government (for address, see page 153).

The Department of Education and Science has also shown itself interested in the cause of international understanding. It has prepared a booklet on *Sources of Information on International and Commonwealth Organisations* (revised annually) which can be ordered by schools; this gives names of associations interested in world affairs and lists teaching aids available. Its pamphlet *Towards World History* is available through H.M.S.O. (Educational Pamphlet No. 52).

Lastly, some of the Universities regularly provide courses in world understanding for teachers. The School of Oriental and African Studies, University of London, for instance, runs an increasingly popular one-term course for teachers (for which, of course, leave of absence has to be granted).

Similarly, books for children about other parts of the world are now much easier to come by than they were only a few years ago. Until comparatively recently, those on Russia, China, and the Far East were particularly rare, so

I should like to mention some of these first. *Visual Histories*, published by Evans, are very useful because they cover in clear, simple form the history of Far Eastern lands such as India and China; the series also deals with Africa and the West Indies. The *Today is History* books, published by Holt-Blond (Blond Educational) are directed at children of about eleven to fifteen, and include volumes on Russia, the U.S.A. and Latin America, as well as on recent European history and on the United Nations. They include, unusually, a book on world religions. Blandford Press produce in their *World History* series an interesting range of books for adolescents, covering world history from the beginnings to modern times. Film-strips and other aids accompany the books.

Longman publish a series, *Making the Modern World*, suitable for older children of average ability. The short, highly illustrated books in the series are grouped by regions and cover Britain, Europe, Asia, Russia, America (including Latin America), and Africa and the Middle East.

Most of the publishers mentioned above publish books on European history. The U.S.A. is now increasingly well catered for. There is *Visual History* (Evans) which goes up to the death of Martin Luther King, while Routledge and Kegan Paul, Faber, and Edward Arnold all produce American histories for schools. In his book *Audio-Visual Material for American Studies* (revised edition), M. Gidley has listed all the available audio-visual aids on American history. It is obtainable from the American Arts Documentation Centre, University of Exeter.

Equally popular these days is the book that approaches recent world history through its problems. For example, there is *Problems of Peace* by Gerald Bailey (Ginn) written for young people of fifteen and upwards. The *World Outlook* study books (Faber) have a similar approach. A selection from their titles demonstrates this: there is *The Unsolved Problem* by M. Dyer (about Southern Africa), *The Hungry World* by A. McKenzie, and *World Co-operation* by J. L. Henderson. A recent book is *The Observer Atlas of World Affairs* (1971), edited by A. Wilson. This depicts in vivid visual form the tensions and conflicts of the modern world.

There are a number of valuable audio and visual aids available for the teaching of world affairs. Pictorial Charts Educational Trust (see page 154) produces excellent, clear charts on up-to-date issues such as Vietnam. So does Educational Productions Ltd (see page 154). B.B.C. and I.T.V. broadcast programmes on world history, such as *Men of our Time* (including Hitler and Roosevelt) by I.T.V. and *History 1917–73* by the B.B.C. Then there are the recorded lectures obtainable on tape from Educational Productions Ltd (in the Sussex Tapes series) on subjects such as the origin of World War II. Lastly there are films, obtainable from the local authority, from sources listed in *Treasure Chest for Teachers*, or from various commercial concerns.

It is perhaps inevitable, with the state that the world is in today, that we should be painfully aware of the distress, bitterness, and apparently insurmountable problems that confront us. One would sometimes think that the most striking feature of the peoples of this world has always been their bitter conflicts. Yet this is to take a narrow view of world history, and by no means a true one, for just as nations have always fought, so they have always met, traded and learnt from each other, and, one is certain, liked each other too. Perhaps we need a new series of world history books showing how this is so. At any rate, to teach world history positively and imaginatively is to teach it hopefully for the future.

I began this book with a consideration of the value of history for the young child. I should like to end it with a plea for the older one. The young child has a need for history, and this need has rarely been explored or even thought about deeply enough. The needs of the adolescent are just as great, and as complex, and these too deserve a consideration that should be just as sensitive. Perhaps this last chapter, on social studies in the schools, a topic which is becoming more and more popular for the school leaver, could serve as a starting-point.

The need of the fourteen or fifteen-year-old that comes most readily to mind is his desire to understand the world in which he lives and his own role in it. It is on this need that the case for introducing him to social studies and the allied disciplines often rests, and with this most people would agree. At the same time one would point out the value of history in this respect to him, for, as one hopes has come through in this chapter, a knowledge of history provides him with a subtle standard by which to judge his own society.

Like the very young child, the adolescent battles to find himself, but he fights a rather different battle in a different way. By the time he reaches his teens a child should have a fully developed historical sense as this is described in Chapter 1. He fully understands that the events that have gone on in the outside world are quite distinct from the inner reality of his own mind; he no longer finds the time-element in history confusing; he has grasped the logic of cause and effect; and he has formed a number of what might be called associative complexes, so that he is able to place together the houses, people, customs and even ways of thought that belong to a particular time in history. What he struggles towards is self-realisation, and this, it is important to realise, in the intellectual as well as in the emotional sense. This is the vital time when he can begin to understand the intellectual disciplines that make up his own culture. There is really no better subject than history to help him here. The intellectual qualities that a study of history develops are important in themselves, such as a grasp of the complex nature of historical truth and the careful judgement that must be exercised in the arriving at it. Added to this, we have the fact that history can also serve as an introduction to nearly all the other disciplines. Many a person's interest in science or French literature has first been awakened by reading about the experiments of the Ancient Greeks, or the court life of seventeenth century France.

As has been remarked already, the older boy or girl is a great talker. A flood of words seems to be released at adolescence, for the very good reason that this is how the adolescent reaches forward intellectually. He has, at last, mastered the ability to grasp concepts through words. This is relevant to the teaching of all subjects, for, in our western culture, most of our ideas are expressed in verbal form. What the older boy or girl needs in the history lesson, is, above all, good books, and many of them. He needs to know how to use a history book properly, using it actively with questions in his mind, and using it creatively, in order to write his own essay. He can enjoy, at this stage, writing his own history, particularly in the form of a local study. In this way he comes to learn something of the craft of history. This is the age too at which boys and girls attain their individual, adult personalities, so that the teacher has a special role to play. He should aim, through his teaching, to encourage the adolescent to find his own individual intellectual style.

This is not to say that the older boy and girl cannot gain greatly from all the other approaches that have been mentioned in this book. In fact, I would make a special plea for their inclusion. The days have gone by, or at least they are going, when the older, academic child was taught history in one way, usually formally, and the younger child was taught it in another, usually child-centred way. Older children, too, need the opportunity to make models, write plays and use technological aids creatively, at least as much as younger ones. In this respect, the secondary schools are learning from the primary. However, ultimately, and in the last resort, the ideas of history are expressed in books.

Perhaps, then, we can now give an answer to the little girl described in Chapter 1 who wanted to know why she had to learn history. It is simply that the educated man or woman can perform any task, however humble, that much better.

Useful addresses for catalogues and information

Film-strips

Educational Audio-Visual Ltd, 30a Drayton Park, London, N5

Educational Productions Ltd,
Bradford Road, East Ardsley, Wakefield, Yorkshire, WF3 2JN

National Audio-Visual Aids Centre, 254–6 Belsize Road, London, NW6

Nicholas Hunter Filmstrips, 40 Richmond Road, Oxford

Rank Film Library,
PO Box 70, Great West Road, Brentford, Middlesex, TW8 9HR

School Broadcasting Council for the United Kingdom,
The Langham, Portland Place, London, W1A 1AA

Sunday Times,★
PO Box 7, Thomson House, 200 Gray's Inn Road, London,WC1X 8EZ

(Film-strips are also issued by certain publishers—for example, Longman Group, Blandford Press—in connection with some of their series.)

Films (addresses for catalogues)

Shell International Petroleum Co.,
Film Library, Shell Centre, London, SE1 7NA

Unilever Film Library, Unilever House, Blackfriars, London, EC4

Petroleum Films Bureau, 4 Brook Street, London, W1

National Coal Board,
Film Library, Hobart House, Grosvenor Place, London, SW1

Games

Priority, Harrison Jones School, West Derby Street, Liverpool 7

Society for Academic Games and Simulations in Education and Training,
5 Errington, Moreton-in-Marsh, Gloucestershire

★(for current affairs film-strips)

Records

B.B.C. Records, The Langham, Portland Place, London, W1A 1AA

Decca Record Co. Ltd, 9 Albert Embankment, London, SE1

Discourses Ltd, High Street, Tunbridge Wells, Kent

Educational Audio-Visual Ltd, 30a Drayton Park, London, N5

Topic Records Ltd, 27 Nassington Road, London, NW3

(Records are also issued by certain publishers—for example, Longman Group —in connection with some of their series.)

Tapes

Educational Productions Ltd,
Bradford Road, East Ardsley, Wakefield, Yorkshire, WF3 2JN

'London Tape', Honor Oak School, Homestall Road, London, SE22

National Audio-Visual Aids Centre, 254–6 Belsize Road, London, NW6

Stagesound (London) Ltd, 14 Langley Street, London, WC2H 9JG

Ordnance Survey historical (and other) maps

Ordnance Survey, Romsey Road, Maybush, Southampton, SO9 4DH

Current events

Atlantic Information Centre for Teachers,
23–5 Abbey House, 8 Victoria Street, London, SW1

Oxfam, 274 Banbury Road, Oxford

Parliamentary Group for World Government,
37 Parliament Street, London, SW1

Sunday Times,*
PO Box 7, Thomson House, 200 Gray's Inn Road, London, WC1X 8EZ

The Times Special Publications, Printing House Square, London, EC4

*(film-strip service)

General

Historical Association, 59A Kennington Park Road, London, SE11

Displays

M. Myers & Son Ltd (for metal fittings)
Vicarage Street, Oldbury, Warley, Worcestershire

Square Tube Systems Ltd (for metal fittings)
Etruria Works, Mount Pleasant, Bilston, Staffordshire

Visual Aids Centre (for pens, glues, mounting papers, etc.)
78 High Holborn, London, WC1

Wiggins Teape (Stationery) Ltd (enquiries about Das and Varni-Das)
Grove Road, Chadwell Heath, Essex, RM6 4XL

Wall charts

Educational Productions Ltd,
Bradford Road, East Ardsley, Wakefield, Yorkshire, WF3 2JN

ESL Bristol Ltd, St Lawrence House, 29–31 Broad Street, Bristol, BS1 2HF

Pictorial Charts Educational Trust, 132 Uxbridge Road, London, W13

Radio and television programmes

B.B.C.:   School Broadcasting Council for the United Kingdom,
             The Langham, Portland Place, London, W1A 1AA

             B.B.C. Television Enterprises,*
             Villiers House, The Broadway, London, W5 2PA

Independent: Independent Television Authority,
             70 Brompton Road, London, SW3

             (and Education Officers of local television companies)

*(for catalogues and programme hire)

Index

original sources:
  aims of using, 59, 64, 70
  definition, 55
  types of, 55–65, 70, 72

'patch' approach, 29–32
practical work:
  criteria of judgement, 51–3
  importance, 37–40
  useful materials, 40, 53–4
  ways of working in the class-room,
    40–51
project work, 113–16

secondary school, *see* adolescents
social studies:
  approaches to teaching, 133–42
  growth in popularity, 125–7

relationship to history as a
  discipline, 127–33
story approach, 22–6
study kits, 65–9, 120–3
syllabus, 35

teacher's role, 100–2, 110–12, 115,
  120, 124
textbook and its use, 26–8

visits, 70–2

wall-charts, 90, 133, 149
work-cards, 61, 120, 123
work-kits, 29, 120–3
world history, 144–50

young children and history, *see* infant
  and junior school; middle school